New York Notary Public Study Guide

Ace the Exam on Your First Try with No Effort | Test Questions, Answer Explanations & Insider Tips to Score a 99% Pass Rate

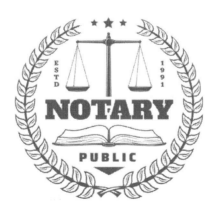

Daniel Shaw

Table of Contents

Introduction

A notary public is a professional who serves as an impartial witness during the signing of important legal documents. Obtaining a notary public commission in New York can unlock numerous career and personal growth opportunities. However, before becoming certified, you must successfully pass the New York Notary Public Exam. This chapter aims to thoroughly explore all aspects of this exam – from its purpose and historical context to the importance of achieving a passing score.

Definition of a Notary Public

A notary public is a professional who acts as an impartial witness during the signing of crucial legal documents. These documents may include contracts, deeds, wills, and various other paperwork requiring verification of identity and signature. Notaries are entrusted with verifying the identities of all parties involved in the transaction and ensuring that each individual comprehends the contents of what they are signing.

Notaries also play a pivotal role in safeguarding against fraud and illegal activities such as money laundering or terrorism financing. They are bound by the rules and regulations outlined in the laws of the state where they practice.

In New York State, aspiring notaries must fulfill specific training requirements before being granted their commission. Once certified, notaries can undertake a variety of responsibilities beyond merely witnessing signatures. These duties may include administering oaths or affirmations to witnesses during depositions or court proceedings.

Becoming a notary public can be an enriching experience, both personally and professionally. It demands attention to detail, effective communication skills, and a steadfast commitment to upholding ethical standards.

Importance of Obtaining a Notary Public Commission in New York

Securing a notary public commission in New York is paramount for establishing credibility and trustworthiness as a professional. In this capacity, individuals serve as impartial witnesses, facilitating the signing of various legal documents, including contracts, affidavits, deeds, and more.

The significance of obtaining a notary public commission cannot be overstated. It unlocks numerous opportunities for career advancement or entrepreneurial pursuits. Notaries play a pivotal role in providing essential services to clients, such as authenticating signatures on crucial documents or witnessing the execution of legal instruments.

Beyond mere recognition by the state government, holding a New York notary public commission can foster strong client relationships, particularly with those who frequently require such services. This, in turn, can lead to enhanced client retention and referrals.

Furthermore, becoming a notary public signifies that individuals have undergone rigorous training and have successfully passed the necessary exams. They possess a deep understanding of the laws governing document authentication and fraud prevention measures, thereby safeguarding the interests of all parties involved in any transaction.

Obtaining a New York notary public commission yields numerous benefits beyond adding another credential to one's resume. It positions individuals as trusted authorities among peers and clients, equipping them with invaluable skills essential for handling crucial documents across various industries. These skills include authenticating signatures on vital legal papers, facilitating business deals, and providing protection against fraudulent activities.

Purpose of the New York Notary Public Exam

The New York Notary Public Exam serves as a vital assessment tool to ensure that individuals seeking a notary public commission possess the requisite knowledge and skills to fulfill their duties effectively. This exam functions as a screening process, evaluating candidates' understanding of legal and ethical responsibilities.

The exam covers a wide range of topics, including identifying document signers, maintaining accurate documentation, and handling sensitive information in compliance with New York State laws governing notarization.

Comprising multiple-choice questions and practical exercises, the exam is conducted under controlled conditions in designated testing centers statewide.

Passing this exam is indispensable for obtaining a notary public commission in New York, as it guarantees that only competent individuals can provide reliable services while adhering to legal standards. Through this stringent process, authorities uphold high standards of professionalism, promoting transparency and accountability among notaries public.

Successfully passing the New York Notary Public Exam confirms an applicant's competence and dedication to upholding legal ethics throughout their career, thereby ensuring the integrity of the notarial profession.

History of Notaries Public in New York

Notaries public have served as crucial components of legal systems for centuries, acting as impartial witnesses to verify the authenticity of important documents during their execution. In New York, notaries have long been pivotal in maintaining the integrity of legal transactions.

The history of notaries public in New York traces back to colonial times when they were appointed by the Governor or Mayor. Records dating as far back as 1665 indicate the authorization of individuals to act as notaries in Manhattan and Albany.

During this era, notaries played a vital role in upholding order within communities by recording significant events such as marriages, births, and deaths.

As New York burgeoned into a bustling commercial hub in the 19th century, the necessity for proper documentation and authentication of legal transactions surged. Consequently, state laws governing notary commissions underwent alterations to meet these evolving demands.

In the contemporary system, aspiring notaries must undergo a rigorous examination covering relevant laws and procedures. Successful completion of this examination ensures that only qualified individuals are entrusted with such critical responsibilities.

The evolution of laws regulating notaries public throughout history has facilitated enhanced protection against fraud and the misuse of power within society.

Evolution of Notary Laws and Regulations in New York

The profession of notary public in New York boasts a rich history dating back to the Dutch colonial era. Over time, regulations governing notaries have adapted to keep pace with societal and technological advancements.

In the mid-19th century, New York mandated that notaries pass an examination before receiving their commissions. This measure was implemented in response to concerns regarding corrupt practices among certain notaries. The examination covered legal principles, oath-taking procedures, and document authentication.

In 2010, New York enacted a law significantly expanding the duties of notaries. This legislation permitted remote online notarization using audio-video technology, marking a significant leap forward in enhancing efficiency and accessibility for individuals and businesses alike.

Present-day notaries public in New York must adhere to stringent ethical guidelines and follow detailed procedures when executing their duties. These regulations serve to ensure the proper authentication of documents and prevent fraud or abuse of power by those holding notarial commissions.

Given the rapid pace of technological advancement, further revisions to the laws governing notaries in New York and beyond are likely. Nevertheless, one constant remains: notaries public play an indispensable role in our legal system by providing impartial verification of essential documents, catering to the needs of individuals requiring passports or marriage certificates, as well as assisting large corporations in swiftly and efficiently handling complex contracts.

Importance of Passing the Exam

Successfully passing the New York Notary Public Exam is paramount for individuals aspiring to become reputable notary public professionals. This examination serves as a crucial gateway to ensure that only competent individuals can carry out the duties of a notary with integrity and professionalism.

Demonstrating your comprehensive grasp of the laws, regulations, and ethical standards governing notarial acts in New York through passing the exam showcases your proficiency in executing essential notarial duties such as administering oaths, certifying documents, and accurately acknowledging signatures without errors.

Additionally, enhancing your professional credibility by passing the exam signals to potential clients or employers your commitment to upholding the responsibilities of a notary public in New York.

Moreover, unlocking numerous career advancement opportunities comes with passing the exam. As a commissioned notary public in New York, you have the flexibility to operate independently, providing services to the community, or seek employment with law firms and other businesses frequently requiring notarized documents.

In summary, passing the New York Notary Public Exam is indispensable for those aiming to establish themselves as competent and trustworthy notary public professionals.

Becoming a notary public in New York holds significant importance for individuals looking to broaden their professional horizons. It offers an avenue to serve the community while supplementing income. The New York Notary Public Exam is meticulously designed to ensure that those receiving this commission are well-versed and qualified to fulfill the role of a notary public.

Requiring thorough preparation, unwavering dedication, and steadfast commitment, passing the New York Notary Public Exam brings substantial rewards as it unveils numerous avenues for career progression. Whether you're gearing up to undertake the exam soon or contemplating a career as a notary public in general, valuable insights into the exam and the profession await you.

Chapter 1

Eligibility Requirements

Are you preparing to take the New York Notary Public exam? Before you delve into your studies, it's important to understand the essential eligibility requirements. These requirements are in place to ensure that only qualified individuals become notaries public, capable of fulfilling their duties with integrity and responsibility. In this chapter, we'll outline the different eligibility criteria for the New York Notary Public Exam, helping you determine if you meet the qualifications. So, let's begin!

Importance of Eligibility Requirements for the New York Notary Public Exam

Eligibility requirements for any professional exam are crucial, and the New York Notary Public Exam is no exception. These requirements serve to maintain high standards of ethics, competence, and professionalism among notaries public. Given their access to sensitive information and involvement in legal procedures, it's imperative that only individuals meeting these criteria are entrusted with such responsibilities.

Meeting these eligibility requirements demonstrates an individual's capability, moral character, and proficiency in performing notarial duties. Additionally, it ensures that notaries public stay abreast of current laws and regulations, thereby providing accurate and reliable services to clients while minimizing errors.

Understanding these eligibility criteria fully is essential for anyone considering taking the New York Notary Public Exam. By meeting these qualifications, you'll have the opportunity to join a respected profession dedicated to serving the community with excellence.

Purpose of Eligibility Requirements

Eligibility requirements are integral to any profession or examination, including the New York Notary Public Exam. Their purpose is to ensure that only suitable candidates take on the responsibilities of a notary public, thereby contributing to a more competent workforce.

Prospective notaries must recognize the significance of meeting these eligibility requirements, as it enables them to uphold integrity in their work and provide valuable services to their communities and businesses.

Minimum Age Requirement

Meeting the minimum age requirement is paramount for those aspiring to become notaries public in New York. This criterion ensures that only mature individuals with adequate life experience can undertake the responsibilities of this role.

The minimum age requirement for the New York Notary Public Exam is eighteen. Applicants must be at least 18 years old to apply for the exam and obtain licensure as a notary public in New York. There is no upper age limit for candidates, but they must be eighteen or older to sit for the examination.

Meeting this eligibility requirement demonstrates maturity and responsibility, essential qualities for every successful notary public. It also ensures that notaries can make sound judgments and conduct their duties with professionalism.

Explanation of the Minimum Age Requirement

The minimum age requirement is a critical aspect of the New York Notary Public Exam's eligibility criteria. It ensures that only individuals who have reached a certain level of maturity can undertake the responsibilities associated with being a notary public.

Applicants must be at least 18 years old to apply for the New York Notary Public Exam. This requirement exists because notaries public play a crucial role in legal documentation and transactions, requiring individuals to demonstrate maturity, responsibility, and accountability in their duties.

It's important to note that meeting the minimum age requirement alone does not guarantee success on the exam or certification as a notary public. Applicants must fulfill all eligibility criteria outlined by law before undertaking the examination.

Before applying for any professional designation, such as becoming a licensed notary public in New York State, it's essential to ensure that you meet all eligibility requirements set forth by the authorities.

Specified Age Limit for the New York Notary Public Exam

The New York Notary Public Exam is a crucial step for individuals aspiring to become notaries public in New York. Among the key eligibility requirements is meeting the specified age limit.

So, what precisely is this age limit? According to the law, individuals must be at least 18 years old to take the exam and become a notary public in New York State. This criterion ensures that those undertaking such a significant responsibility possess the necessary maturity to handle it effectively.

It's essential to emphasize that there is no upper age limit for taking the exam. As long as all other eligibility requirements are met, individuals can take the exam at any point.

If you're wondering why this requirement is vital, consider this: being a notary public entails substantial responsibilities. Individuals assuming such duties should have attained an appropriate level of maturity and accountability. Hence, fulfilling this age requirement is crucial.

In summary, to successfully apply for and pass the New York Notary Public Exam, ensure that you fulfill all eligibility criteria, including meeting the minimum age requirement specified by law.

Importance of Meeting the Minimum Age Requirement

Meeting the minimum age requirement is paramount for anyone seeking to take the New York Notary Public Exam. This requirement, mandated by law, cannot be waived, making it an essential aspect of eligibility.

The specified age limit for the New York Notary Public Exam is 18 years old or older. Individuals under 18 are ineligible to take the exam, regardless of their qualifications or experience.

Meeting this requirement ensures that candidates have attained the necessary level of maturity and responsibility required for the position. Notaries public bear significant duties such as verifying identities, witnessing signatures, and affirming oaths, all of which demand sound judgment and integrity.

Furthermore, meeting the minimum age requirement demonstrates candidates' respect for the regulations governing public service positions like that of a notary public. It showcases their ability to adhere to legal requirements essential for serving in an official capacity.

Meeting the minimum age requirement indicates that candidates possess the essential qualities expected of every reputable notary public in New York State: trustworthiness, reliability, and accountability.

Residency and Citizenship Requirements

Fulfilling residency and citizenship requirements is another crucial aspect of eligibility for the New York Notary Public Exam. Regarding residency, applicants must be residents of New York State, meaning they must have a physical address in one of the five boroughs or any county in New

York State.

Meeting these residency and citizenship requirements helps prevent fraudulent activities by providing additional safeguards against unqualified individuals becoming notaries public.

Residency Requirement for New York State

Meeting the residency requirement for New York State is a prerequisite for taking the New York Notary Public Exam. This requirement ensures that only individuals with ties to and knowledge about the state can notarize documents within its borders.

If you plan on applying for the exam, ensure that you can prove your residency through documentation such as utility bills or driver's licenses. Simply having a mailing address in New York does not necessarily meet this requirement.

It's also important to note that if you move out of state after becoming a notary, your commission may no longer be valid, and you will need to reapply once you establish residency again in New York State.

Fulfilling the residency requirement is crucial to becoming a licensed notary public in NY, so it should be carefully considered before applying.

Citizenship Requirement for New York State

To become a New York Notary Public, you must be a citizen of the United States or a legal permanent resident. If you are an immigrant with permanent residency status, you must provide proof of your immigration status during the application process.

It's important to emphasize that being a citizen or legal permanent resident does not automatically qualify you as a notary public in New York State. You must still meet all other eligibility requirements and pass the required exam.

If you need further clarification about your citizenship status, it's best to double-check before applying for the exam. You don't want to waste time and money on an application that may ultimately be denied due to citizenship issues.

Remember, being a notary public is an important responsibility that demands honesty and integrity. Therefore, it is sensible that only citizens and legal residents are eligible for this role within New York State.

Criminal Background Checks in Notary Public Applications

Before individuals can become Notary Publics in New York State, they must meet several eligibility requirements, one of which is a criminal background check. This process involves fingerprinting and an FBI criminal history record search to ensure that only trustworthy individuals are granted the authority to notarize legal documents. While having a criminal record does not automatically disqualify someone, certain offenses such as fraud, forgery, perjury, embezzlement, and other crimes involving dishonesty or moral turpitude may lead to denial or revocation of their commission. It's crucial for applicants to disclose all past convictions on their application and provide necessary documentation or explanations to support their eligibility. Passing the criminal background check is a fundamental step in becoming a Notary Public in New York State as it helps maintain public confidence in the integrity and trustworthiness of our state's notaries.

Types of Offenses That May Disqualify Applicants

Understanding what types of offenses may disqualify an individual from becoming a notary public is essential. Any felony conviction automatically disqualifies an applicant, including crimes such as murder, rape, arson, and robbery. Additionally, any misdemeanor or lesser offense involving dishonesty or moral turpitude may also result in disqualification. Examples of misdemeanors that could lead to disqualification include theft, forgery, perjury, embezzlement, or fraud, while lesser offenses could be traffic violations or disorderly conduct charges. However, each case is evaluated individually, and having a past conviction does not necessarily disqualify someone from taking the notary public exam. State officials consider each case on its own merits, taking into account the circumstances surrounding the offense.

Clearance Requirements for Successful Candidates

Successful candidates must meet clearance requirements to become a New York State Notary Public, ensuring they possess good moral character and have no disqualifying criminal history. The clearance process begins with submitting fingerprints for a background check, either electronically or via ink card submission, which law enforcement agencies forward to the Division of Criminal Justice Services. Candidates will then receive notification regarding any potential areas of concern on their report and be given an opportunity to contest incorrect information before further steps are taken. While successful completion of this stage does not guarantee immediate approval, it ensures that eligible applicants' applications will continue processing promptly. Once cleared through all stages successfully, candidates can proceed to take the notary public exam.

Other Eligibility Criteria

In addition to citizenship and criminal background checks, there are other eligibility criteria individuals must meet to become notary publics in New York. One such criterion is educational requirements. Applicants must be at least 18 years old and have obtained a high school diploma or equivalent. If high school was not completed, passing the General Educational Development (GED) test suffices. While a college degree is not mandatory, it may enhance an applicant's credentials, particularly degrees in related fields such as law or business administration. However, these degrees are optional for becoming a successful notary public.

Good Moral Character

Having good moral character is another crucial eligibility criterion for becoming a New York Notary Public. This entails having a record of behaving honestly and ethically. State officials consider factors such as criminal history, financial responsibility, and reputation in the community when evaluating an applicant's moral character. While not every mistake or misstep automatically disqualifies an applicant, serious offenses like fraud or embezzlement may raise concerns. Even if a criminal history does not automatically disqualify someone, it is considered during the application process. Therefore, maintaining honesty and integrity in all aspects of life is vital for aspiring notaries public. Ultimately, demonstrating honesty, trustworthiness, and reliability over time increases the likelihood of qualifying for this important role.

Notary Public Application Process in New York State

The process of becoming a notary public in New York State involves several important steps that candidates must complete diligently. Let's delve into each step with clarity and precision.

Step 1: Application Submission

The initial step entails obtaining an application form either from the Division of Licensing Services or by downloading it from their official website. Applicants are required to complete the application form accurately, ensuring all fields are filled out correctly. Alongside the application, a fee of $60 must be submitted, along with proof of identity such as a valid driver's license or passport.

Step 2: Education Requirement

Candidates must demonstrate their knowledge by completing at least six hours of approved education in notary law and procedures. This educational component is crucial as it equips candidates with the necessary understanding of their responsibilities and obligations as notaries.

Step 3: Examination

Upon processing of the application, candidates deemed eligible will be notified to proceed with the examination. The examination assesses candidates' understanding of proper identification procedures, document signing requirements, and ethical considerations relevant to notarial duties.

Step 4: Seal Acquisition

Successful candidates who pass the examination must obtain an official seal, which should be filed with their respective county clerk's office. This seal is a symbol of authority and signifies the notary's capacity to perform notarial acts.

Step 5: Commencement of Notarial Services

Following the acquisition of the official seal and filing it with the county clerk's office, candidates are then authorized to commence offering notarial services to the public. It's imperative for notaries to adhere to legal standards and ethical principles in the execution of their duties.

Conclusion

In conclusion, aspiring notaries in New York State must diligently navigate through the application process, ensuring compliance with all requirements and standards set forth by the Division of Licensing Services. By adhering to these steps with meticulous attention to detail, candidates can embark on a career path as responsible and trusted notary public officials, serving their communities with integrity and professionalism.

Chapter 2

How to Pass the Exam?

Many students aspire to excel in the New York Notary Exam, yet for many, the task can seem daunting. Fear not, as we're here to provide you with comprehensive guidance. This chapter is designed to equip you with effective strategies and techniques to ensure success on your exam journey. From setting achievable goals to utilizing appropriate study materials and seeking guidance from seasoned notaries, let's embark on the path to preparing you for triumph in the New York Notary Exam.

Setting Goals for Exam Success

Establishing clear goals is fundamental to conquering the New York Notary Exam. It's imperative to have a precise understanding of what you aim to accomplish and how you plan to achieve it. Begin by setting realistic and specific objectives, such as dedicating a certain number of hours to study each day or completing a fixed number of practice questions weekly. Ensure that your goals are measurable to monitor your progress effectively. Additionally, devise a timeline for reaching your goals, working backward from your desired exam date and breaking down your study plan into manageable milestones. Remember, the essence of goal-setting lies in fostering motivation rather than discouragement. Avoid setting yourself up for failure with unrealistic expectations or overly aggressive timelines. Celebrate your progress by acknowledging small victories along the way. Reward yourself upon reaching a milestone or completing a section of study material. Maintaining a positive outlook will sustain your motivation throughout the preparation process.

Study Tips and Strategies

Preparing for the New York Notary Exam demands a combination of knowledge, skill, and strategy. Given the extensive content of the exam, it's easy to feel overwhelmed. Hence, adopting effective study tips and strategies is paramount to success.

Familiarize Yourself with Exam Content

Prior to sitting for the New York Notary Exam, acquaint yourself with the content you'll encounter. Understanding the exam's requirements is crucial, including the rules and regulations governing notarial acts and the duties expected of a notary public. Moreover, grasp the format of the exam, which comprises multiple-choice questions covering various topics such as legal concepts, ethics, notarial acts, and procedures. Being aware of the number of questions and time allocations will aid in pacing your study sessions. Stay abreast of any updates or changes in notarial services regulations, as these may impact the exam content. Familiarizing yourself comprehensively with all aspects of the New York Notary Exam will boost your confidence and enhance your chances of success.

Create a Study Plan

Crafting a well-structured study plan is instrumental in acing the New York Notary Exam. Whether you feel overwhelmed or require organization, follow these tips for devising an effective study plan:

Allocate dedicated time for studying each day or week to maintain consistency and deter procrastination.

Prioritize study materials, focusing on areas that require improvement. Utilize practice tests and quizzes to assess your knowledge and identify weaknesses.

Break down complex topics into manageable sections for better comprehension. For instance, if real estate law poses a challenge, dissect it into specific aspects like mortgages or property ownership.

Incorporate diverse learning techniques such as visual aids or group discussions to enhance engagement and retention.

Remain flexible with your study plan while staying committed to your goals. With dedication and organization, passing the New York Notary Exam is undoubtedly achievable.

Utilize Study Materials and Resources

Leveraging appropriate study materials and resources is indispensable for success in the New York Notary Exam. Fortunately, a plethora of options are available to aid your preparation:

Notary exam prep books offer comprehensive coverage of exam content, practice questions, and valuable tips. Popular choices include "Passing the Notary Public Exam" by Angelo Tropea and the "New York Notary Public Law Manual."

Online courses provide interactive lessons, quizzes, and videos to facilitate understanding of key concepts. Consider reputable platforms like the National Notary Association's Online NY Notary

Course or Kaplan Real Estate Education's Online NY State-Approved Notary Public Training.

Engage in study groups or seek guidance from experienced tutors to supplement your preparation. These avenues offer additional support and opportunities for clarifying complex topics.

Make use of free resources such as practice tests provided by the state or review materials available at your local library.

Harnessing these resources alongside a structured study plan significantly enhances your likelihood of passing the New York Notary Exam.

Focus on Key Topics and Concepts

Concentrating on essential topics and concepts is pivotal during exam preparation, as it fosters deeper understanding and improves your chances of success. Key areas to prioritize include:

Notarial acts: Understand the nature, usage, and proper execution of notarial acts, including acknowledgments and jurats.

Ethical responsibilities: Familiarize yourself with the ethical obligations of a notary public in New York, emphasizing honesty, integrity, and compliance with relevant laws and regulations.

New York state laws: Acquaint yourself with laws governing notarization in New York, including document requirements, authorized individuals for notarial acts, and record-keeping obligations.

By focusing your studies on these critical areas and regularly testing your knowledge with sample questions, you'll bolster your readiness for the exam. Remember, practice makes perfect!

In conclusion, by adhering to these meticulously crafted strategies and techniques, you'll be well-equipped to tackle the New York Notary Exam with confidence and proficiency. Stay committed, stay focused, and success will undoubtedly be within reach.

Practicing with Sample Questions

Practice with sample questions is an essential aspect of preparing for the New York Notary Exam. This practice aids in acquainting yourself with the exam's format and types of questions, enabling you to identify your strengths and weaknesses. The more you engage in practice, the better equipped you'll be for the exam day.

Numerous online resources offer sample questions similar to those found on the New York Notary Exam. You can commence by searching for free practice tests or downloading study guides containing practice questions.

When practicing with sample questions, it's crucial to simulate test conditions as closely as possible. Time yourself and approach each question methodically, akin to how you would in the actual exam. This approach helps in building confidence and reducing anxiety on the test day.

Furthermore, thoroughly reviewing both correct and incorrect answers after completing each set of sample questions is vital. Analyze why certain answers were incorrect, their related concepts, and how you could arrive at the correct answers instead.

Seeking guidance from experienced notaries or other professionals while practicing with sample questions can prove invaluable. Their insights may aid in understanding complex topics or areas where you encounter the most difficulty during preparation.

Guidance from Experienced Notaries

One of the most effective ways to prepare for the New York Notary Exam is by seeking guidance and advice from experienced notaries. These individuals have already traversed the exam process and can offer valuable insights into what to expect on exam day.

Consider reaching out to local notary associations or attending networking events to connect with other professionals in the field. Additionally, finding a mentor who can provide one-on-one coaching as you study for the exam can be immensely beneficial.

Receiving feedback from those who have successfully passed the exam can help identify areas where you need more practice and provide tips and strategies for improving your performance.

Time Management during the Exam

Effective time management is critical for passing the notary exam in New York. The exam comprises multiple sections, including true/false, multiple-choice, and essay questions, necessitating wise allocation of time for each section.

Reading and understanding instructions carefully is paramount for success in the notary exam. Take the time to thoroughly read through all instructions before commencing any section, ensuring comprehension of requirements such as time limits, word counts, or specific formatting.

If certain terms or concepts are unclear, seek clarification from the proctor before starting the exam to avoid confusion during the test.

Dividing your total exam time based on the number of sections or questions can aid in effective time management. Allocate more time to sections with higher marks or those requiring more complex answers. Having a clear plan for time allocation ensures adequate time is dedicated to each section, preventing rushing through any part of the exam.

Answer Easier Questions First

Initiating with answering questions you find more accessible and can confidently tackle is an effective time management strategy. This approach allows you to build momentum and confidence as you progress through the exam. By swiftly answering the simpler questions, you accumulate points and foster a positive mindset, which can be advantageous when addressing more challenging questions later on. This strategy also helps in avoiding getting stuck on difficult questions early in the exam, saving valuable time.

Review Your Answers if Time Permits

Utilize any remaining time to review your answers once you've completed all questions. During the review process, check for errors, incomplete answers, or areas needing clarification. Ensure no questions have been missed or simple mistakes made due to oversight or time constraints. While reviewing, strike a balance between thoroughness and avoiding excessive time spent on each answer. Focus on identifying any significant errors or omissions that can be rectified within the available time.

Stress Management during the Exam

Experiencing stress during exams is normal, but implementing stress management techniques can create a more positive and calmer exam environment. Adapt these strategies to your preferences and needs to reduce stress and optimize your performance during the New York Notary Exam.

Practice Relaxation Techniques Before the Exam

Engaging in relaxation techniques before the exam can help calm your mind and reduce stress levels. Effective methods include deep breathing exercises, progressive muscle relaxation, and meditation. These practices alleviate anxiety, enhance focus, and promote a sense of calmness. Find a technique that works best for you and incorporate it into your pre-exam routine to prepare yourself mentally and emotionally.

Use Positive Affirmations and Self-Talk to Boost Confidence

Positive affirmations and self-talk significantly influence your mindset and confidence during the exam. Affirmations are positive statements you repeat to yourself, such as "I am well-prepared and capable of succeeding in this exam." They counteract negative self-doubt and bolster self-confidence by reinforcing positive thoughts. Remind yourself of your strengths, knowledge, and past successes to boost belief in your abilities.

Stay Focused on the Task at Hand and Avoid Distractions

Maintaining focus is crucial for stress management during the exam. Eliminate or minimize distractions that can divert attention and increase anxiety. Find a quiet, comfortable environment free from interruptions or disturbances. Put away unnecessary electronic devices and study materials that may tempt you to lose focus. Remind yourself of the task's importance and remain fully engaged, concentrating on one question at a time.

Conclusion

In conclusion, passing the New York Notary Exam requires a comprehensive approach involving effective study habits, efficient time management, and stress management techniques. By diligently preparing, familiarizing yourself with the exam content, creating a study plan, and seeking guidance from experienced notaries, you can establish a solid foundation for success. Effective time management, maintaining calmness, and staying focused during the exam will enhance your performance. By adhering to these strategies and approaches, you can confidently approach the exam and increase your likelihood of success. Remember to stay motivated, maintain a positive mindset, and believe in your abilities throughout the process.

Chapter 3

Notary Exam New York Format and Content

Are you considering becoming a notary public in New York? Embarking on this path is indeed a significant step toward a rewarding career. However, before you can notarize documents, you must successfully pass the Notary Exam in New York. This examination is designed to evaluate your understanding of the state laws and regulations governing the responsibilities of notaries. But what precisely does this exam entail? In this guide, we'll comprehensively explore the format, content, and significance of the Notary Exam in New York. So, let's delve into it!

The Various Types of Notary Exams

There exist different versions of notary exams depending on the state and jurisdiction. In New York, there are primarily two types of exams: the traditional written exam and an online proctored exam.

The traditional written exam is a paper-based assessment comprising multiple-choice questions. Typically conducted at designated testing centers statewide, this exam covers various topics, including legal terminology, ethical conduct, witnessing signatures, and identifying signers.

Conversely, the online proctored exam is internet-based, allowing candidates to undertake it from any location with a stable internet connection. Unlike the traditional format, this exam incorporates video conferencing to monitor candidates throughout the assessment.

Each exam format presents its advantages and drawbacks. While the online proctored exam offers convenience and flexibility, some individuals may prefer the traditional written format due to familiarity or concerns regarding technology issues during remote testing.

Understanding the Exam Format

The Notary Exam in New York comprises both written and practical components. The written segment consists of multiple-choice questions assessing the examinee's comprehension of various notarial law and practice topics.

Structurally, the exam comprises two sections, each containing 50 questions, totaling 100 questions. It's noteworthy that the content covered may vary based on the county where the exam is administered, as well as updates or revisions made by relevant state authorities.

To prepare effectively for the Notary Exam, prospective candidates can consult study materials such as handbooks and online resources provided by state agencies. Additionally, some opt for training courses offered by private institutions or individuals specializing in notarial law and procedure.

Familiarizing oneself with the exam's format is paramount for success on test day. Thus, candidates are advised to thoroughly acquaint themselves with the content and structure of each section before undertaking the exam.

Types of Questions

The Notary Exam in New York assesses candidates' knowledge across various domains pertinent to notarial practices. It encompasses multiple-choice questions, true/false queries, scenario-based assessments, and short-answer tasks.

Multiple-choice questions necessitate candidates to select one correct answer from a list provided. These questions may range from straightforward to intricate, demanding critical thinking skills for accurate responses.

True/false questions require candidates to discern the veracity of statements presented. Due diligence is crucial, as minor details can significantly impact the accuracy of responses.

Scenario-based questions prompt candidates to analyze specific situations and formulate appropriate responses based on their understanding of notarial practices.

Short-answer questions entail providing concise yet comprehensive responses, covering all essential information.

Acquainting oneself with these diverse question types aids in effective exam preparation, ensuring candidates are equipped to tackle the assessment confidently.

Time Limit Considerations

Time management plays a pivotal role in the Notary Exam in New York. Candidates are allotted two hours to complete the assessment, which may initially seem sufficient but can swiftly elapse if not managed judiciously.

Maintaining awareness of one's progress and pacing oneself accordingly is essential. Spending excessive time on individual questions or sections risks running out of time before completing the entire exam.

To mitigate the risk of time constraints, candidates are advised to allocate specific timeframes for each task. For instance, setting aside around 30 minutes for review upon answering all questions in each section helps ensure comprehensive coverage within the stipulated timeframe.

Vigilantly monitoring the time throughout the exam and devising a strategic plan beforehand facilitates optimal time utilization while comprehensively addressing the requirements of each question.

Number of Questions and Passing Criteria

The number of questions in the Notary Exam varies based on the chosen format. For the online exam, candidates must complete 50 multiple-choice questions within the allotted two-hour timeframe. Conversely, the written exam administered by the Department of State Division of Licensing Services NY typically comprises 80-100 questions.

It's imperative to note that passing either exam format necessitates achieving a minimum score of 70% (35/50) or higher in correct answers.

In conclusion, preparing for the Notary Exam demands diligence and dedication. With ample preparation, including thorough study of relevant materials and practice tests, aspiring notaries can bolster their chances of success. Remember, becoming a notary public is an investment in both personal growth and community service. By diligently adhering to legal provisions and regulations, you can embark on a fulfilling journey of serving your fellow citizens as a trusted notary public in New York.

Notary Public Laws and Regulations in New York

In New York, the laws and regulations surrounding notary publics are intricate and comprehensive. A notary public must possess a deep understanding of both federal statutes and the specific mandates outlined by the state of New York.

At its core, the role of a notary public is to act as an impartial witness to the signing of crucial legal documents, including wills, deeds, and contracts. Their primary responsibility is to ensure that each party voluntarily signs the document without any form of coercion.

Overview of Notary Public Laws in New York

In New York, notary publics operate within the framework of both federal and state laws and regulations. Their fundamental duty is to serve as impartial witnesses during the signing of significant legal documents.

Federal laws governing notaries public encompass various aspects such as identification requirements, record-keeping obligations, and prohibitions against fraudulent activities. These laws are designed to uphold integrity and accountability within the notarial process.

New York state laws specific to notaries public outline the prerequisites for obtaining a notary commission, which includes educational and testing criteria. Furthermore, these laws delineate the scope of practice for notaries in New York, specifying the types of documents they are authorized to witness or certify.

A thorough understanding of these laws is indispensable for individuals aspiring to become successful notaries public in New York. Adhering closely to legal guidelines ensures the maintenance of client trust while delivering valuable services to the community.

Federal Laws and Regulations Governing Notaries Public

Federal laws and regulations play a crucial role in ensuring that notaries fulfill their duties consistently, ethically, and within the bounds of the law. The primary federal legislation relevant to notarization is the Notary Act of 1950, which sets forth minimum standards for the appointment and commissioning of notaries public.

Under federal law, individuals seeking to become notaries must meet specific eligibility criteria, including being at least 18 years old, free of felony convictions or disqualifying misdemeanors, completing a state-sanctioned application process, and passing an exam on basic legal principles.

Moreover, federal law mandates that all documents requiring authentication by a notary must be signed in their presence. It also imposes stringent record-keeping requirements to ensure transparency and accountability in notarial transactions.

It is important to note that while many states adhere to similar guidelines outlined in federal law, there may be variations in rules across jurisdictions.

New York State Laws and Regulations Specific to Notaries Public

New York state laws and regulations establish particular requirements for individuals seeking to become notaries public. Key prerequisites include being at least 18 years old, a legal resident of New York State, and proficient in English reading and writing.

Additionally, applicants must have a clean criminal record, demonstrating honesty and integrity. They are also required to provide personal references from reputable sources to attest to their moral character.

Once appointed as notaries public in New York, individuals must adhere to strict guidelines for their duties, including accurately identifying signers and maintaining thorough records of all transactions conducted.

Notaries public in New York are prohibited from providing legal advice or acting as attorneys unless duly licensed. Failure to comply with these regulations may result in disciplinary action.

Understanding Critical Legal Provisions and Requirements

As a notary public in New York, it is imperative to comprehend the essential legal provisions and requirements governing your profession. This understanding will help you navigate potential legal challenges and provide clients with high-quality service.

One crucial aspect of this comprehension involves recognizing the various documents that necessitate notarization, such as affidavits, deeds, contracts, and powers of attorney.

Moreover, being familiar with proper identification methods for signers is paramount. Verifying the identity of signatories through government-issued IDs or other approved means is essential before notarizing their signatures.

Additionally, awareness of specific protocols when dealing with vulnerable populations, such as minors or the elderly, is vital. Extra precautions are necessary when handling documents involving individuals with diminished capacity due to age-related illnesses like dementia.

It is essential to stay abreast of changes and updates in notarial practices as each state may have distinct rules and regulations. Remaining informed will enable you to provide accurate services while avoiding potential fines or penalties for non-compliance.

In summary, possessing comprehensive knowledge of critical legal provisions and requirements is indispensable for achieving success as a Notary Public in New York.

Duties and Powers of a Notary Public in New York

In New York, the role of a notary public encompasses several essential duties and powers, all of which are pivotal in upholding legal standards and ensuring the integrity of documents and transactions.

Role and Responsibilities of a Notary Public in New York

The primary responsibility of a notary public in New York is to verify the voluntary nature of signatories' signatures on documents, ensuring they are not under any form of duress or coercion. Additionally, notaries are tasked with administering oaths or affirmations when necessary for legal proceedings and maintaining accurate records of all transactions they oversee.

Moreover, in New York State, notaries are authorized to certify copies of specific documents like birth certificates and diplomas, as well as issue apostilles to authenticate the validity of official records for international use. It's crucial to emphasize that while notaries can assist with completing forms and provide guidance on filling in blanks, they cannot offer legal advice.

Furthermore, notaries play a crucial role in identifying signers and ensuring their comprehension of the documents they are signing before affixing their signature. This underscores the significant responsibility placed upon notaries, necessitating strict adherence to codes of conduct and ethical standards mandated by state laws and regulations.

Powers and Authority Conferred upon Notaries Public

As a notary public in New York, you are endowed with specific powers and authority to execute your duties effectively. Foremost among these is the responsibility to verify the authenticity of signatures on legal documents, thereby confirming the identity of signatories.

Notaries public are also empowered to administer oaths or affirmations to individuals making statements under penalty of perjury, as well as certify copies of original documents such as birth certificates or passports. Additionally, they play a pivotal role in witnessing and attesting to the execution of legal documents like deeds or contracts, ensuring all parties understand the terms outlined therein.

Furthermore, notaries have the authority to issue subpoenas for witnesses when mandated by law, compelling their testimony or provision of evidence. However, it's imperative to exercise these powers judiciously and ethically, recognizing the weight of the responsibility entrusted to notaries public.

Limits and Restrictions on Notarial Duties

Despite the authority conferred upon notaries, there are inherent limits and restrictions to their duties. Notaries in New York cannot provide legal advice or prepare legal documents for others, nor can they perform notarial acts in cases involving fraud or coercion.

Additionally, notaries are prohibited from notarizing their own signature or that of individuals with whom they share a close personal relationship. These limitations are essential to maintain impartiality and prevent conflicts of interest, safeguarding the integrity of the notarial process.

Understanding the Significance of the Notarial Function

The role of a notary public extends beyond mere documentation; it is fundamental to ensuring the authenticity and legality of transactions within society. Notarization serves as a bulwark against fraud and disputes, instilling trust in communities, businesses, and legal systems alike.

Central to the significance of the notarial function is its role in verifying identities, confirming signatures, and certifying documents, thereby mitigating potential risks associated with improperly executed transactions. Moreover, many governmental agencies mandate notarized documents for various purposes, underscoring the indispensability of notarial services in bureaucratic processes.

Ultimately, by upholding ethical principles and professional standards, notaries public contribute to the maintenance of trust and reliability within the legal framework. Recognizing the importance of their role ensures the continued efficacy and credibility of notarial services in facilitating secure and transparent transactions.

Ethics and Professional Responsibilities in New York

As a notary public in New York, upholding ethical standards and professionalism is paramount to fulfilling your duties effectively. Several key principles govern professional conduct for notaries, ensuring integrity and trustworthiness in their interactions with clients and the public.

Professional Conduct and Behavior Expected from Notaries Public

Maintaining impartiality, punctuality, and clear communication are fundamental aspects of professional conduct for notaries. Notaries must conduct themselves with professionalism and ensure that clients understand each step of the notarial process, thereby fostering trust and confidence in their services.

Moreover, dressing appropriately and handling clients' personal information with confidentiality and discretion are imperative. By demonstrating empathy and providing excellent customer service, notaries can forge lasting relationships built on trust and reliability.

Confidentiality and Privacy Obligations in Notarial Practices

As a notary public in New York, you are entrusted with handling sensitive and confidential information during notarial acts. This information may encompass personal details concerning the parties involved, including their full names, addresses, dates of birth, or social security numbers.

It is imperative to uphold your duty to maintain confidentiality and privacy rigorously throughout the notarization process. This involves ensuring that any information obtained during the process is securely stored and protected from unauthorized access.

To achieve this, implementing physical safeguards such as securely locking up documents and utilizing password-protected computer systems is essential. Additionally, remaining vigilant against cyber threats, such as phishing scams or other online attacks, is crucial to safeguarding your clients' data.

While maintaining confidentiality is paramount, there may be instances where disclosure of certain information is mandated by law or legal proceedings. In such cases, it is imperative to follow proper procedures for disclosure while still respecting the privacy rights of your clients.

By prioritizing confidentiality and privacy and taking proactive measures to protect sensitive information, you demonstrate professionalism and integrity as a trusted notary public in New York.

Managing Conflicts of Interest and Preserving Impartiality

Becoming a notary public in New York requires adherence to rigorous ethical standards and principles, including maintaining confidentiality, managing conflicts of interest, and preserving impartiality.

The role of a notary public is integral to our legal system, as it ensures the authenticity of important documents and transactions. Consequently, notaries must approach their responsibilities with the utmost seriousness.

By understanding the boundaries and ethical requirements of their role, notaries can uphold professional standards, ensure privacy obligations are met, and manage conflicts of interest with impartiality. This commitment contributes to the efficient and effective administration of justice.

Whether you are considering a career as a notary public in New York or seeking to deepen your understanding of this vital profession, remember that trustworthiness is fundamental to success in this role.

Notarial Procedures and Practices in New York

As a notary public in New York, you will perform various notarial acts, including administering oaths and affirmations, taking acknowledgments, and certifying copies of documents. It is essential to understand the legal requirements and procedures associated with each type of activity to execute them accurately.

Guidelines for Executing Various Notarial Acts

Performing notarial acts entails a significant responsibility for every notary public in New York. Different types of documents require distinct approaches based on their nature.

One common notarial act is acknowledgment, which involves verifying the signer's identity and ensuring their voluntary signing of the document. The notary must also confirm the identification and willingness of any required witnesses.

Jurats, on the other hand, require the signer to swear or affirm under oath the accuracy of the document's contents. The notary must administer this oath or affirmation while verifying the identities of all involved parties.

Certified copies involve verifying that a photocopy or scanned copy matches the original document. Notaries must carefully scrutinize both copies before certifying them as accurate duplicates.

Additionally, specialized notarial acts such as protests and depositions are used in specific situations. Every notary public in New York must comprehend the nuances of each type and apply the appropriate procedure accordingly to fulfill their duties accurately and efficiently.

Proper Completion of Notarial Certificates and Forms

As a Notary Public in New York, meticulous completion of notarial certificates and documents is paramount to ensuring the validity and legal standing of the notarization process. The notarial certificate serves as tangible proof that the notarization was conducted, underscoring the importance of accurate completion.

The specific contents of the certificate and form depend on the type of notarial act performed, whether it be an acknowledgment, jurat, or certified copy. Essential details such as dates, names of signers and witnesses, and document titles must be meticulously included during the completion of these forms.

It's crucial to acknowledge that errors in this process can render the notarization invalid or inadmissible in court proceedings. Therefore, meticulous attention to detail is imperative, and every element must undergo thorough triple-checking before finalizing the documents.

Moreover, Notaries must ensure they utilize approved certificates/forms sanctioned by state government agencies, as each state imposes varying requirements concerning format and content.

By adhering to meticulous standards and following all legal procedures, Notaries safeguard against potential legal challenges in the future, ensuring the integrity of the notarization process.

Record-keeping and Maintenance of Notarial Journals or Registers

The meticulous record-keeping and maintenance of notarial journals or registers are foundational responsibilities for a Notary Public in New York. These records serve as permanent documentation of the Notary's notarial acts, serving as crucial evidence in legal proceedings.

The journal or register should comprehensively detail each transaction, including the date and time, type of activities performed, names and addresses of all involved parties, and any identification used for identity verification. Additionally, it's imperative to record any fees charged for services rendered.

Notaries must securely maintain their journals or registers to prevent unauthorized access, which includes storing them in a locked cabinet when not in use and restricting access solely to authorized individuals.

In addition to meticulous record-keeping, Notaries must comply with relevant laws governing record retention periods. In New York State, Notaries are legally required to retain their journals or registers for a minimum of ten years after the last entry.

By diligently adhering to these standards and legal requirements, New York Notaries fulfill their responsibilities as impartial witnesses while safeguarding against potential legal liabilities.

Safeguarding Notary Seals, Stamps, and Tools of the Trade

Protecting notary seals, stamps, and other tools of the trade is paramount for Notaries Public in

New York to uphold the integrity of their role. Here are some key tips for safeguarding these essential items:

1. Always securely store seals and stamps when not in use, preferably in a locked cabinet or drawer.
2. Never lend out seals or stamps to anyone other than yourself, as they are strictly for use by the Notary Public.
3. Ensure that unused papers with pre-printed certificates or forms are securely stored to prevent unauthorized use.
4. Safeguard access to your journal or register where each notarial act is recorded to prevent tampering or unauthorized access.
5. In the event of loss or suspected theft of any notary items, promptly report the incident to the appropriate authorities and take preventative measures to mitigate future risks.

By adhering to these precautions, Notaries Public can minimize the risk of identity fraud and unauthorized use while upholding compliance with New York state regulations governing their practice.

Conclusion

Becoming a Notary Public in New York entails more than just passing an exam; it requires a deep understanding of proper procedures and practices to ensure the integrity of notarial acts. Notaries must be well-versed in their responsibilities regarding identification, verification, certificate completion, record-keeping, and safeguarding tools.

Adherence to these regulations is essential for preventing fraud and protecting the parties involved in transactions requiring notarization. Aspiring Notaries should dedicate ample time to thoroughly study the format and content covered in the exam to ensure proficiency in their role.

Obtaining a Notary Public Commission in New York signifies a commitment to upholding the highest standards of integrity and professionalism in facilitating legal and financial transactions. By following best practices and legal guidelines, Notaries Public play a vital role in ensuring the trustworthiness and legality of essential documents and transactions within their community.

Chapter 4

Notary Public Responsibilities and Practices

Introduction to Notary Public in New York

Are you acquainted with the term "Notary Public"? If not, let's delve into the world of Notary Public in New York. In legal transactions, having a witness to verify the legitimacy of signatures on essential documents is crucial. This is where Notary Publics come into play. They act as impartial witnesses, ensuring that legal documents are authentic and legally binding. In this chapter, we will explore the roles, responsibilities, official duties, and powers granted by law to Notary Publics in New York.

Importance of Notarial Services in Legal Transactions

The significance of notarial services in legal transactions cannot be overstated. These services form the backbone of various agreements, contracts, and deals, providing an extra layer of security and authenticity.

One vital aspect that renders notarial services indispensable is their role in preventing fraud. A Notary Public's primary duty is to act as an impartial witness, verifying the identities of all parties signing a document. This minimizes the chances of forgery or other fraudulent activities during the completion of legal transactions.

Another crucial area where notaries play a significant role is in upholding contractual obligations among involved parties. By verifying signatures and acknowledging consent, notaries facilitate smooth execution while deterring disputes regarding legitimacy or agreed-upon terms.

Moreover, notarial acts help maintain public trust in essential documents such as deeds, trusts, wills, and powers of attorney. As these documents carry weighty consequences for individuals and businesses alike, it is necessary to have them validated by an objective third party – hence the role played by Notary Publics.

In summary, notarial services add credibility and reliability to legal transactions, providing concrete proof of their validity and enforceability.

Roles and Responsibilities of a Notary Public

Notary Publics play a critical role in ensuring the legality and integrity of various legal transactions. Their primary responsibilities include:

- Verifying the identity of signatories.
- Witnessing signatures.
- Administering oaths or affirmations.
- Certifying copies of essential documents.

In addition to these duties, Notary Publics must also maintain accurate records of all notarial acts performed.

Official Duties and Powers Granted to Notaries in New York

The official duties and powers given to notaries in New York are extensive. Notaries can administer oaths and affirmations, take acknowledgments and proofs of deeds or other instruments, witness signatures, certify copies of documents, and more.

One of the most significant responsibilities of a Notary Public is to verify the identity of signers. This includes checking identification documents such as driver's licenses or passports to ensure they match the name on the signed record.

Notaries are also responsible for ensuring that all parties understand what they are signing. They must ensure that everyone involved comprehends the implications and consequences of signing a legal document.

In addition to these core responsibilities, notaries in New York have additional powers. For example, they can issue subpoenas for witnesses who must testify in court cases related to their official duties.

Furthermore, notaries may also be called upon to provide services outside their traditional scope. For instance, some may offer translation services or assist with real estate transactions by explaining relevant laws or procedures.

Notaries are essential in ensuring legal transactions are adequately conducted in New York State. Their official duties help safeguard against fraud while promoting transparency and accountability.

Safeguarding the Integrity of Notarial Acts

As a Notary Public, one of the primary responsibilities is to ensure that notarial acts maintain their integrity and authenticity. This involves safeguarding legal documents from fraud or any other illegal activities.

One way to protect against fraudulent activity is by verifying the identity of signers before performing any notarial act. A Notary should always ask for government-issued identification and verify that the signer's signature matches what is on their ID.

Another important aspect of safeguarding notarial acts is ensuring that all parties involved are acting of their own free will and without coercion or duress. A Notary must be vigilant in detecting signs of pressure or influence on a signer and may refuse to perform a notarization if they suspect foul play.

It is also essential for a Notary Public to keep accurate records of all notarial transactions performed, including the date, location, type of document signed, and names of all parties involved. These records help provide evidence if there are questions about whether proper procedures were followed during the signing process.

Maintaining an unwavering commitment to ethical behavior while conducting official duties as a Notary Public ensures trustworthiness within our legal system.

Ensuring Compliance with Legal Requirements and Regulations

As a Notary Public in New York, one critical responsibility is ensuring compliance with legal requirements and regulations. Notaries must have a vast knowledge of state laws governing notarial acts to avoid potential legal issues.

Notaries are required to verify the identity of signatories before performing any notarial act. In addition, they must confirm that signatories willingly sign documents without coercion or duress. Compliance with these requirements ensures that records produced by the Notary Public will be legally binding and enforceable.

It is also essential for notaries to maintain up-to-date records and document all transactions accurately. This includes recording the date, time, location, type of transaction performed, and names of parties involved in each transaction.

Furthermore, notaries must stay informed about updates or changes in legislation affecting their practice. They should continuously educate themselves on new laws and regulations regarding notarial acts in New York State.

Ensuring compliance with legal requirements is integral to maintaining trust in the integrity of notarized documents. Adhering strictly to regulatory standards while keeping abreast of relevant legislative developments impacting their work as a Notary Public helps prevent errors or omissions during transactions, consequently reducing disputes arising from non-compliance with statutory provisions.

Common Notarial Acts and Procedures

Notarial acts and procedures refer to the duties a notary public in New York can perform. These include acknowledging signatures, certifying copies of original documents, administering oaths, and protesting negotiable instruments.

Acknowledgments

Acknowledgments are one of the most common notarial acts performed by Notary Publics in New York. This act is a process used to verify a signer's identity and confirm their willingness to sign a document.

During an acknowledgment, the signer must appear before the Notary Public and affirm that they signed the document willingly and without coercion. The Notary then verifies the signer's identity through government-issued or other forms of identification.

A critical aspect of acknowledgments is that they require impartiality on behalf of the Notary Public. They cannot have any personal interest in or gain from witnessing an admission - their role is strictly to verify identity and ensure that proper procedures are followed.

Notably, acknowledgments differ from jurats as oath-taking is optional during this process. However, it's still essential for acknowledges to understand what they're signing and for whom it may concern.

Acknowledgments are crucial in protecting individuals' rights when signing legal documents, ensuring accuracy while maintaining integrity throughout New York State.

Jurats

Jurats are among the most common notarial acts performed by Notary Publics in New York. It serves as a form of verification for an individual's sworn statement or oath. Jurats are utilized when a document requires confirmation that its contents are true and accurate to the best knowledge of the signer.

The person signing must take an oath or affirmation before the Notary Public. The Notary will then sign and stamp their official seal on the document indicating that they have witnessed and verified the signature and statements made by the individual.

Notaries must be familiar with state laws regarding jurats, including proper wording requirements for oaths and affirmations. Additionally, it is crucial to verify that signers understand what they are swearing or affirming to avoid any potential legal issues.

Ultimately, practicing precision and attention to detail during every aspect of conducting jurats helps ensure accuracy and reliability in notarial services provided by New York Notaries Public.

Copy Certifications

Copy certifications are another vital notarial act that a Notary Public in New York is responsible for performing. This type of notarization involves verifying that a photocopy of an original document is true and accurate.

In other words, if someone needs to provide a copy of their driver's license or passport to submit with an application, the Notary Public can certify that the document is authentic.

To perform this service, the individual must present the original document and its photocopy to the Notary Public. The Notary will then compare both documents to ensure they match ideally before placing their official certification on the photocopy.

It's important to note that only certain documents qualify for copy certification services. For example, legal documents such as birth certificates or marriage licenses cannot be copied and certified by a Notary Public in New York due to privacy concerns.

Copy Certifications are essential for anyone who wants proof of authenticity when presenting copies of important documents and play an integral role in protecting against fraud and forgery.

Oaths and Affirmations in Notarial Practice

In the realm of notarial acts, oaths and affirmations hold significant importance, as they entail solemn promises or declarations made by individuals. These acts find common application in legal proceedings and contracts, binding the individual taking the oath or affirmation by law to fulfill their commitment.

When administering an oath, a notary public must ensure that the individual comprehends the gravity of their promise. It is imperative to confirm that they fully understand the terms before proceeding. Conversely, an affirmation dispenses with any religious connotations, allowing individuals who prefer not to swear on sacred texts to express their sincerity in their own words.

Notaries Public play a crucial role in reviewing documents necessitating oaths and affirmations, verifying identities through photo identification cards before commencing with these pivotal procedures. Maintaining impartiality throughout these processes is essential, irrespective of individuals' actions or statements during these moments.

Protests of Negotiable Instruments

As a Notary Public in New York, one may encounter responsibilities such as handling protests of negotiable instruments, which denote rights to payment, including checks or promissory notes.

A protest constitutes a formal declaration made by a holder of a dishonored instrument, indicating non-payment upon presentation. This situation may arise due to insufficient funds in the maker's account or other issues with the instrument itself. Notaries may be called upon to witness and certify these protests, meticulously documenting details such as the presenter's name and reasons for dishonor, while maintaining impartiality and accuracy.

Tips for Providing Effective Notarial Services

Effective notarial services are paramount to safeguard the integrity and authenticity of legal documents. Here are some guidelines to ensure efficient and reliable notarial services:

Understanding the Importance of Impartiality and Integrity

Notaries must grasp the significance of impartiality and integrity in executing their duties. Impartiality necessitates avoiding conflicts of interest or situations compromising objectivity. For instance, abstaining from providing services for transactions where personal gain is at stake is advisable.

Integrity entails adherence to state laws governing document preparation and identification requirements. Additional training on proper conduct during official duties can bolster these values, ensuring high-quality service delivery devoid of favoritism.

Maintaining Confidentiality and Privacy

Preserving confidentiality and privacy is fundamental for Notaries Public in New York. All client-related information must be kept confidential, including details about notarized documents and signers' identities. Secure storage of documents and sharing information only with authorized individuals are imperative practices.

Given the sensitive nature of legal matters handled by notaries, such as wills or trusts, upholding confidentiality is paramount to prevent potential harm. By prioritizing client privacy, notaries foster trust and uphold the integrity of their profession.

By adhering to these principles, Notaries Public in New York uphold professionalism, ensuring the trustworthiness of notarial acts and maintaining the sanctity of legal processes.

Understanding relevant laws, regulations, and procedures

As a Notary Public in New York, it is imperative to have a comprehensive understanding of the pertinent laws, regulations, and procedures governing your role. This knowledge ensures that you can fulfill your duties effectively and ethically within the legal framework.

New York state has specific rules governing notarization, particularly for documents such as wills, real estate transactions, and adoption papers. Familiarizing yourself with these requirements is essential to safeguarding the interests of all parties involved.

Moreover, notaries must adhere to federal laws alongside state regulations. For instance, verifying the identity of signers using government-approved forms of identification is a federal requirement. This underscores the importance of staying updated on both state and federal mandates to ensure compliance and legality in every transaction.

Understanding the proper procedures for various notarial acts, such as acknowledgments and jurats, is equally crucial. Failure to follow these procedures meticulously can lead to legal consequences or the invalidation of documents. Therefore, maintaining a thorough grasp of these protocols is paramount for upholding the integrity of your role as a Notary Public.

In essence, possessing a comprehensive knowledge of relevant laws and regulations empowers Notary Publics in New York to execute their responsibilities diligently while upholding legal standards.

Effective communication and customer service skills

In addition to legal proficiency, effective communication and exceptional customer service are integral aspects of being a Notary Public in New York.

Clear communication is vital for guiding clients through the notarial process and addressing any inquiries or concerns they may have. Active listening, clear articulation, and patience are key components of effective communication, especially when explaining legal concepts to clients unfamiliar with the terminology.

Moreover, cultural sensitivity plays a significant role in client interactions. Recognizing and respecting cultural differences fosters trust and understanding, contributing to positive client experiences.

Exemplary customer service entails demonstrating professionalism, respect, and empathy towards all clients. Regardless of their background or circumstances, every individual should be treated with dignity and courtesy. Transparency regarding fees and charges is essential, ensuring clients are fully informed about the costs involved in notarization services.

Furthermore, punctuality and flexibility are paramount in accommodating clients' needs. Arriving on time for appointments and being responsive to unforeseen circumstances demonstrate reliability and dedication to customer satisfaction.

Ultimately, effective communication and exceptional customer service are pivotal for building trust and fostering long-term relationships with clients, thereby enhancing your reputation within the community.

Ensuring meticulous record-keeping and documentation

Another critical responsibility of Notaries Public in New York is maintaining meticulous record-keeping and documentation practices.

This involves accurately recording all notarial acts and associated fees, establishing a systematic approach that suits both your preferences and the needs of your clients. Whether you opt for digital or paper records, the key is to maintain organized files that are easily accessible and secure.

When completing notarial acts, thorough documentation is essential. This includes recording the date, time, and details of the transaction, as well as verifying the identity of the signers and documenting the forms of identification used.

Furthermore, maintaining detailed records of client communications ensures transparency and accountability. Documenting all interactions regarding appointments, inquiries, or clarifications regarding documents helps uphold professionalism and integrity in your practice.

By adhering to meticulous record-keeping and documentation procedures, you instill confidence in both yourself and your clients, knowing that every transaction is handled with precision and complies with state regulations.

Challenges and Legal Concerns Encountered by Notary Publics in New York

Being a Notary Public in New York presents several challenges and legal considerations. Notaries are tasked with verifying the identities of individuals signing documents, administering oaths, and certifying copies of essential paperwork. However, not all clients readily provide the necessary information, complicating these tasks.

Fraud Prevention and Identity Verification

One of the primary responsibilities of a Notary Public is to prevent fraud and ensure the accurate identification of all parties involved in a transaction. This entails verifying the authenticity of signers and validating their identity through recognized identification documents such as passports or driver's licenses.

Notaries must remain vigilant in detecting fraudulent activities, recognizing common red flags like incomplete documents, unusual client requests or behaviors, and discrepancies in provided information.

To prevent fraud, notaries must strictly adhere to state laws and guidelines, maintaining detailed transaction records and ensuring signers declare their willingness to sign under oath, without coercion.

Utilizing technology, such as electronic notarization services, can further enhance fraud prevention efforts by employing secure digital signature technologies for identity verification purposes.

Dealing with Difficult or Uncooperative Clients

Notaries in New York may encounter clients who are uncooperative, which can hinder the notarization process. Despite these challenges, maintaining professionalism and providing excellent customer service is crucial.

Handling demanding clients requires patience and clear communication. Explaining the necessity of specific procedures or regulations in simple terms can help alleviate client concerns.

Offering alternative options, such as mobile notarization services or rescheduling appointments, may improve cooperation with difficult clients. Notaries must prioritize flexibility and convenience while upholding ethical standards and legal requirements.

Handling Complex or Unusual Notarial Acts

Managing complex or unusual notarial acts demands expertise, attention to detail, and familiarity with various notarial procedures. Notaries must stay updated on relevant laws and regulations to ensure compliance and proficiency in their roles.

These acts may include administering oaths, certifying copies of documents, witnessing the signing of wills and trusts, performing marriage ceremonies, among others.

By continuously updating their knowledge and communication skills, notaries can effectively navigate challenging notarial tasks and ensure the proper execution of legal transactions.

Compliance with Changing Laws and Regulations

Notaries in New York must stay abreast of evolving laws, regulations, and guidelines governing notarial acts to remain compliant and avoid legal repercussions. This necessitates ongoing education, participation in professional development programs, and engagement with relevant professional organizations.

Liability and Legal Risks

Notaries bear significant responsibility for certifying document authenticity, making errors or misconduct potentially costly. To mitigate liability risks, notaries must exercise due diligence, maintain accurate records, and obtain appropriate liability insurance.

By prioritizing accuracy, professionalism, and adherence to ethical standards, notaries can minimize legal risks and uphold the integrity of the notarial process in New York.

Conclusion

In conclusion, the responsibilities of a notary public in New York encompass crucial duties aimed at ensuring the authenticity and accuracy of legal documents. Notaries play a pivotal role in upholding the integrity of the legal system by verifying signatures, administering oaths, and certifying the proper execution of various legal instruments. Their diligent record-keeping, adherence to laws and regulations, and effective communication with clients are essential for delivering effective notarial services.

However, New York notaries also face challenges and legal complexities, including potential liability for errors, adherence to stringent regulations, and staying abreast of evolving laws. Despite these challenges, dedicated New York notaries contribute to a reliable and trustworthy judicial system.

Indeed, the role of a notary public in New York extends beyond mere verification of signatures and oath administration. They serve as pillars of trust in legal transactions, ensuring documents are not only authentic but also compliant with the law. This responsibility is critical in a legal framework heavily reliant on written documentation for conveying rights, entitlements, and obligations.

Given the gravity of their role, New York notaries must adhere to strict ethical standards and maintain impartiality. They serve as the first line of defense against fraud and forgery, with their ability to discern signature authenticity and signatories' intent being crucial in preventing legal misconduct.

Furthermore, the ever-evolving nature of law necessitates that New York notaries commit to lifelong learning. Continuous education is vital for navigating the complexities of legal documents and understanding the evolving legal landscape.

Additionally, New York notaries must balance their legal obligations with the need for accessibility and efficiency. They must efficiently manage their time and resources to serve a diverse clientele, often under tight deadlines. This balance is particularly crucial in a bustling and diverse city like New York, where the demand for notarial services spans various individuals and institutions.

Chapter 5

Practice Test

1. What is the primary role of a Notary Public?

  a) To provide legal advice
  b) To witness and authenticate signatures
  c) To enforce laws and regulations
  d) To represent clients in court

2. Which jurisdiction does a Notary Public operate within?

  a) Global jurisdiction
  b) Federal jurisdiction
  c) State jurisdiction
  d) Local jurisdiction

3. What is the purpose of a Notary Public's jurisdiction?

  a) To handle criminal cases
  b) To handle civil lawsuits
  c) To provide notarial services
  d) To administer oaths in court

4. In which country does a Notary Public's jurisdiction lie?

  a) United States
  b) Canada
  c) United Kingdom
  d) Mexico

5. Can a Notary Public authenticate signatures outside their jurisdiction?

- a) Yes, always
- b) No, never
- c) Yes, under certain conditions
- d) No, only attorneys can do so

6. Which of the following is a responsibility of a Notary Public?

- a) Providing legal advice
- b) Making court judgments
- c) Witnessing the signing of documents
- d) Drafting legal contracts

7. Is a Notary Public responsible for determining the validity of a document's content?

- a) Yes, always
- b) No, never
- c) Yes, in certain situations
- d) No, only attorneys can do so

8. Can a Notary Public refuse to provide services if there are conflicts of interest?

- a) Yes, always
- b) No, never
- c) Yes, in certain situations
- d) No, only attorneys can do so

9. Which of the following documents can a Notary Public authenticate?

- a) Birth certificates
- b) Marriage licenses
- c) Passports
- d) Signatures on legal documents

10. What is the primary purpose of a Notary Public's seal or stamp?

- a) To endorse legal documents
- b) To indicate the expiration date of the commission
- c) To authenticate the Notary Public's signature
- d) To provide a unique identification number

11. Can a Notary Public notarize a document without the signatory being physically present?

- a) Yes, always
- b) No, never
- c) Yes, in certain situations

d) No, only attorneys can do so

12. Which level of government grants the authority to individuals to become Notaries Public?

a) Federal government
b) State government
c) Local government
d) Judicial system

13. Can a Notary Public provide legal advice or services?

a) Yes, always
b) No, never
c) Yes, in certain situations
d) No, only attorneys can do so

14. What is the term of office for a Notary Public in most states?

a) 1 year
b) 2 years
c) 4 years
d) 6 years

15. Can a Notary Public charge fees for their services?

a) Yes, always
b) No, never
c) Yes, within certain limits set by law
d) No, only attorneys can charge fees

16. Can a Notary Public notarize a document in a language they do not understand?

a) Yes, always
b) No, never
c) Yes, if a translator is present
d) No, only attorneys can do so

17. Is a Notary Public required to maintain a record book of notarized documents?

a) Yes, always
b) No, never
c) Yes, within certain limits set by law
d) No, only attorneys are required to do so

18. Can a Notary Public notarize their signature?

a) Yes, always

b) No, never

c) Yes, in certain situations

d) No, only attorneys can do so

19. Do a Notary Public has the authority to refuse to notarize a document if it contains blank spaces?

a) Yes, always

b) No, never

c) Yes, within certain limits set by law

d) No, only attorneys can do so

20. Is a Notary Public responsible for verifying the accuracy of information provided in a document?

a) Yes, always

b) No, never

c) Yes, in certain situations

d) No, only attorneys can do so

21. Can a Notary Public provide their services to family members or close relatives?

a) Yes, always

b) No, never

c) Yes, in certain situations

d) No, only attorneys can do so

22. Can a Notary Public authorize to refuse to notarize a document if the signatory is under the influence of drugs or alcohol?

a) Yes, always

b) No, never

c) Yes, within certain limits set by law

d) No, only attorneys can do so

23. Is a Notary Public required to keep their official seal or stamp secure?

a) Yes, always

b) No, never

c) Yes, within certain limits set by law

d) No, only attorneys are required to do so

24. Can a Notary Public certify a copy of a document?

a) Yes, always

b) No, never

c) Yes, in certain situations

d) No, only attorneys can do so

25. Can a Notary Public authority refuse to notarize a document if the signatory does not understand the content?

a) Yes, always

b) No, never

c) Yes, within certain limits set by law

d) No, only attorneys can do so

26. Can a Notary Public notarize their own spouse's signature?

a) Yes, always

b) No, never

c) Yes, in certain situations

d) No, only attorneys can do so

27. Can a Notary Public notarize a document if the signatory does not have identification?

a) Yes, always

b) No, never

c) Yes, within certain limits set by law

d) No, only attorneys can do so

28. Can a Notary Public provide services outside their home state?

a) Yes, always

b) No, never

c) Yes, within certain limits set by law

d) No, only attorneys can do so

29. Can a Notary Public backdate a notarial act?

a) Yes, always

b) No, never

c) Yes, in certain situations

d) No, only attorneys can do so

29. Can a Notary Public notarize a document if they have a personal interest in the transaction?

a) Yes, always

b) No, never

c) Yes, in certain situations

d) No, only attorneys can do so

30. Which of the following is a primary form of identification accepted by a Notary Public in New York?

   a) Social Security card
   b) Credit card
   c) Birth certificate
   d) Driver's license

31. When verifying a signatory's identification, a Notary Public should:

   a) Accept any form of identification presented,
   b) Compare the signature on the identification document with the signature on the notarized document,
   c) Ignore the identification altogether,
   d) Only accept identification issued by the Notary Public Association

32. New York Notary Publics can rely solely on personal knowledge of the signatory's identity without any identification documents.

   a) True
   b) False

33. If a signatory does not possess any valid identification documents, the Notary Public can:

   a) Refuse to notarize the document,
   b) Accept an affidavit from the signatory as proof of identity,
   c) Notarize the document based on personal knowledge alone,
   d) Accept a witness statement from another individual

34. In New York, which is NOT an acceptable secondary form of identification?

   a) U.S. military ID card
   b) Passport
   c) Employee ID card
   d) Utility bill

35. A Notary Public should refuse to notarize a document if:

   a) The signatory provides an expired identification document,
   b) The signatory does not speak fluent English,
   c) The signatory has a different physical appearance than the photo on the identification document,
   d) The signatory insists on using a non-English signature

36. New York Notary Publics are required to keep a record of the identification presented by signatories.

    a) True

    b) False

37. In New York, how long should a Notary Public maintain a record of the identification presented by a signatory?

    a) not legally required to keep a record book or journal of notarial acts

    b) 1-year

    c) 3 years

    d) 5 years

38. The identification record maintained by a Notary Public should include the following:

    a) The signatory's social security number,

    b) The signatory's home address,

    c) The type of identification presented,

    d) The Notary Public's observations of the signatory

39. A Notary Public should refuse to notarize a document if:

    a) The signatory is unable to provide a valid identification document,

    b) The signatory is in a hurry,

    c) The signatory refuses to answer personal questions,

    d) The signatory has a different hairstyle than the photo on the identification document

40. Which of the following is an acceptable form of identification for a non-U.S. citizen signatory in New York?

    a) Foreign driver's license

    b) Foreign passport

    c) Foreign student ID card

    d) Birth certificate

41. A Notary Public in New York can rely on expired identification documents.

    a) True

    b) False

42. If a signatory is physically unable to sign a document, the Notary Public can:

    a) Sign on behalf of the signatory,

    b) Accept a mark or signature made by a witness on behalf of the signatory,

    c) Notarize the document without any signature,

    d) Refuse to notarize the document

43. In New York, a Notary Public can refuse to notarize a document if:

   a)   The document contains sensitive information,
   b)   The document is in a foreign language,
   c)   The Notary Public knows the signatory personally,
   d)   The signatory's identification document appears altered or forged

44. When verifying a signatory's identification, a Notary Public should examine the following:

   a)   Only the front side of the identification document,
   b)   Only the back side of the identification document,
   c)   Both the front and back sides of the identification document
   d)   None of the above.

45. A Notary Public can use their personal identification documents to verify the signatory's identity.

   a)   True
   b)   False

46. Which of the following identification documents is NOT commonly accepted by a Notary Public in New York?

   a)   State-issued identification card
   b)   Tribal identification card
   c)   Library card
   d)   U.S. passport

47. What should a Notary Public do if they suspect the identification document presented by a signatory is fraudulent?

   a)   Notarize the document anyway to avoid conflict
   b)   Report the suspected fraud to the appropriate authorities
   c)   Request an additional form of identification from the signatory
   d)   Confront the signatory about the suspected fraud

48. New York Notary Publics are authorized to notarize documents outside New York State.

   a)   True
   b)   False

49. How can a Notary Public verify the validity of a foreign identification document?

   a)   Conduct an online search for the document's format and security features
   b)   Request the signatory to provide a second form of identification issued in the United States
   c)   Consult with a legal expert
   d)   Accept the identification document without further verification

50. Which of the following is NOT an acceptable form of identification for a signatory who is visually impaired?

    a) Braille identification card

    b) Identification document with a photo and a tactile feature

    c) Identification document with an audio recording of the signatory's personal information

    d) None of the above

51. New York Notary Publics must keep a logbook of their notarizations.

    a) True

    b) False

52. In New York, a Notary Public should include the signatory's identification information in the notarial certificate for:

    a) Acknowledgments

    b) Jurats,

    c) Oaths and affirmations,

    d) All of the above.

53. Suppose a signatory's identification document does not contain a photograph. In that case, the Notary Public should:

    a) Request the signatory to provide a photograph,

    b) Refuse to notarize the document,

    c) Accept the identification document if it meets all other requirements

    d) Use their judgment to assess the signatory's identity.

54. New York Notary Public can accept expired passports as a valid form of identification.

    a) True

    b) False

55. A Notary Public should refuse to notarize a document if:

    a) The signatory's identification document does not match the name on the document notarized,

    b) The signatory refuses to pay the notarization fee,

    c) The signatory's identification document is laminated,

    d) The signatory arrives late to the appointment

56. In New York, if a signatory presents a foreign passport as identification, the Notary Public should:

    a) Refuse to accept the foreign passport and request a different form of identification,

    b) Notarize the document based on the personal knowledge of the signatory,

c) Only accept the foreign passport if the U.S. Customs and Border Protection has stamped it

d) Consult with a legal expert to ensure compliance with New York regulations

Answer: Consult with a legal expert to ensure compliance with New York regulations

57. Which of the following is an example of a credible identifying witness in New York?

a) A close friend of the signatory

b) A family member of the signatory

c) A neutral third party who knows both the signatory and the Notary Public

d) The Notary Public's co-worker

58. New York Notary Publics must undergo training on proper identification procedures.

a) True

b) False

59. What should a Notary Public do if they suspect a signatory is impersonating another person?

a) Notarize the document anyway to avoid conflict

b) Ask the signatory to provide additional identification documents

c) Refuse to notarize the document and report the suspicion to the appropriate authorities

d) Confront the signatory about the suspicion

60. What is the purpose of authenticating a document?

a) To validate its content

b) To provide legal advice

c) To enforce laws and regulations

d) To notarize the document

61. Which of the following documents requires authentication by a Notary Public?

a) Personal letters

b) Public announcements

c) last will

d) Internal company memos

62. Can a Notary Public authenticate a document that contains blank spaces?

a) Yes, always

b) No, never

c) Yes, under certain conditions

d) No, only attorneys can do so

63. When authenticating a document, what is the role of a Notary Public?

    a) To determine its legal validity

    b) To ensure its accuracy and completeness

    c) To provide legal advice on its content

    d) To draft the document

64. Which of the following is NOT a joint document requiring authentication?

    a) Powers of attorney

    b) Contracts and agreements

    c) Business invoices

    d) Loan document

65. Can a Notary Public authenticate a document written in a foreign language?

    a) Yes, always

    b) No, never

    c) Yes, with proper translation

    d) No, only attorneys can do so

66. What is the process of authenticating a document called?

    a) Certification

    b) Notarization

    c) Validation

    d) Authentication

67. Can a Notary Public authenticate a copy of an original document?

    a) Yes, always

    b) No, never

    c) Yes, under certain conditions

    d) No, only attorneys can do

68. Can a Notary Public authenticate a document that is signed electronically?

    a) Yes, always

    b) No, never

    c) Yes, under certain conditions

    d) No, only attorneys can do so

69. What information should include when authenticating a document?

    a) Notary Public's contact information

    b) Date and location of notarization

    c) Signature of the document signer

d) All of the above

70. Can a Notary Public authenticate a document if the signatory is mentally incapacitated?

a) Yes, always
b) No, never
c) Yes, under certain conditions
d) No, only attorneys can do so

71. Is it necessary to have witnesses present when authenticating a document?

a) Yes, always
b) No, never
c) Yes, under certain conditions
d) No, only attorneys can do so

72. Can a Notary Public authenticate an incomplete or missing information document?

a) Yes, always
b) No, never
c) Yes, under certain conditions
d) No, only attorneys can do so

73. Can a Notary Public authenticate a document if the signatory refuses identification?

a) Yes, always
b) No, never
c) Yes, under certain conditions
d) No, only attorneys can do so

74. Can a Notary Public authenticate a document that has been altered or tampered with?

a) Yes, always
b) No, never
c) Yes, under certain conditions
d) No, only attorneys can do so

75. Can a Notary Public authenticate a signed document using a digital signature?

a) Yes, always
b) No, never
c) Yes, under certain conditions
d) No, only attorneys can do so

76. Can a Notary Public authenticate a document written in handwriting that is difficult to read?

    a) Yes, always

    b) No, never

    c) Yes, under certain conditions

    d) No, only attorneys can do so

77. Can a Notary Public authenticate a document if the signatory is visually impaired?

    a) Yes, always

    b) No, never

    c) Yes, under certain conditions

    d) No, only attorneys can do so

78. Can a Notary Public authenticate a document that contains false information?

    a) Yes, always

    b) No, never

    c) Yes, under certain conditions

    d) No, only attorneys can do so

79. Can a Notary Public authenticate a document signed with a mark instead of a signature?

    a) Yes, always

    b) No, never

    c) Yes, under certain conditions

    d) No, only attorneys can do so

80. Can a Notary Public authenticate a document that has expired or is no longer valid?

    a) Yes, always

    b) No, never

    c) Yes, under certain conditions

    d) No, only attorneys can do so

81. Can a Notary Public authenticate a document if the signatory is not physically present?

    a) Yes, always

    b) No, never

    c) Yes, under certain conditions

    d) No, only attorneys can do so

82. Can a Notary Public authenticate a document if the signatory is a minor?

    a) Yes, always

    b) No, never

c) Yes, under certain conditions

d) No, only attorneys can do so

83. Can a Notary Public authenticate a document if the signatory does not understand the language?

a) Yes, always

b) No, never

c) Yes, under certain conditions

d) No, only attorneys can do so

84. Can a Notary Public authenticate a document if the signatory refuses to sign it?

a) Yes, always

b) No, never

c) Yes, under certain conditions

d) No, only attorneys can do so

85. Can a Notary Public authenticate a document if the signatory is under the influence of drugs or alcohol?

a) Yes, always

b) No, never

c) Yes, under certain conditions

d) No, only attorneys can do so

86. Can a Notary Public authenticate a document if there is a dispute over its content?

a) Yes, always

b) No, never

c) Yes, under certain conditions

d) No, only attorneys can do so

87. Can a Notary Public authenticate a document if the signatory cannot sign?

a) Yes, always

b) No, never

c) Yes, under certain conditions

d) No, only attorneys can do so

88. Can a Notary Public authenticate a document if the signatory is not of sound mind?

a) Yes, always

b) No, never

c) Yes, under certain conditions

d) No, only attorneys can do so

89. Can a Notary Public authenticate a document with a missing or incorrect notarial certificate?

   a) Yes, always
   b) No, never
   c) Yes, under certain conditions
   d) No, only attorneys can do so

90. Can a Notary Public authenticate a document if the signatory is not mentally competent?

   a) Yes, always
   b) No, never
   c) Yes, under certain conditions
   d) No, only attorneys can do so

91. Which of the following is true regarding the form of a notarial document?

   a) It must be handwritten in blue ink.
   b) It must be typewritten or printed in black ink.
   c) Two witnesses must sign it.
   d) It must be written on legal-sized paper.

92. Which of the following requires in the heading of a notarial document?

   a) The date of the document's execution.
   b) The signature of the notary public.
   c) The county where the document executes.
   d) The notary public's seal.

93. In New York, a notarial document must include

   a) A statement of acknowledgment.
   b) A statement of authorization.
   c) A statement of indemnification.
   d) A statement of intent.

94. The notarial document must contain the expiration date of the notary's commission.

   a) True
   b) False

95. Which of the following requires a notarial document to be valid?

   a) The document must notarize within 24 hours of its execution.
   b) At least three witnesses must sign the document.
   c) The document must stamp with the notary public's thumbprint.
   d) The signer must acknowledge the document.

96. When a notarial document includes a jurat, it means:

a) The document must notarize in the presence of a judge.

b) A jury must sign the document.

c) The document must contain a sworn statement.

d) A notary's attorney must sign the document.

97. Which of the following requires in the notarial certificate of acknowledgment?

a) The notary public's personal identification number.

b) The notary public's email address.

c) The notary public's commission expiration date.

d) The notary public's seal.

98. In New York, a notary public must attach a _____ to each notarial act performed.

a) Copy of the signer's identification document.

b) Receipt of payment.

c) Certificate of registration.

d) Jurisdictional stamp.

99. A notarial document can back dated earlier than the execution date.

a) True

b) False

100. Which of the following is NOT required in the notarial certificate of acknowledgment?

a) The signature of the notary public.

b) The county where the notary's commission is registered.

c) The date of the acknowledgment.

d) The printed name of the notary public.

101. What is the purpose of a notarial certificate of protest?

a) To record a formal declaration of non-payment or dishonor of negotiable instruments.

b) To acknowledge the authenticity of a public official's signature.

c) To certify the execution of a power of attorney.

d) To authenticate the transfer of real property.

102. Which of the following requires a notarial document to be executed by a corporate entity?

a) The signature of the CEO.

b) The corporate seal.

c) The signature of a licensed attorney.

d) The signature of a notary public from a different state.

103. A notarial certificate of protest can issue by a notary public who is also an attorney.

    a) True

    b) False

104. What is the purpose of a notarial certificate of qualification?

    a) To acknowledge the execution of a will.

    b) To certify the authenticity of a passport.

    c) To authorize the formation of a business entity.

    d) To confirm the qualifications of a notary public.

105. Which of the following is NOT a required element in the notarial certificate of protest?

    a) The date and place of protest.

    b) The signature of the notary public.

    c) The reason for the protest.

    d) The name of the person presenting the document for protest.

106. A notarial document must always sign in the presence of a notary public.

    a) True

    b) False

107. Which of the following is NOT required in the notarial qualification certificate?

    a) The notary public's commission expiration date.

    b) The date of the qualification.

    c) The county where the qualification took place.

    d) The notary public's signature.

108. What is the purpose of a notarial certificate of proof?

    a) To acknowledge the authenticity of a deed.

    b) To certify the completion of a notarial act.

    c) To validate the identity of a witness.

    d) To prove the execution of a document.

109. A notarial certificate of proof requires for all documents related to real estate transactions.

    a) True

    b) False

110. Which of the following is required in the notarial certificate of proof?

    a) The notary public's seal.

    b) The notary public's social security number.

c) The notary public's email address.

d) The notary public's thumbprint.

111. In New York, a notary public may not notarize a document if:

a) The document is in a foreign language.

b) The document needs to be completed.

c) The document is more than ten pages long.

d) The document contains a typographical error.

112. A notary public can notarize their signature.

a) True

b) False

113. Which of the following is required in the notarial certificate of proof of execution?

a) The notary public's personal phone number.

b) The date of the document's execution.

c) The notary public's bank account number.

d) The notary public's occupation.

114. What is the purpose of a notarial certificate of oath?

a) To certify the authenticity of a birth certificate.

b) To acknowledge the execution of a power of attorney.

c) To administer an oath or affirmation.

d) To endorse the transfer of a motor vehicle.

115. If a notary public attaches a certificate of authentication, they may charge an extra fee.

a) True

b) False

116. Which of the following is NOT a required element in the notarial certificate of oath?

a) The date of the oath.

b) The signature of the notary public.

c) The printed name of the person taking the oath.

d) The notary public's social security number.

117. What is the purpose of a notarial certificate of consent?

a) To acknowledge the execution of a contract.

b) To certify the authenticity of a marriage certificate.

c) To obtain permission for a minor to travel internationally.

d) To authorize the adoption of a child.

118. A notary public may notarize a document that contains blank spaces.

   a) True
   b) False

119. Which of the following is required in the notarial certificate of consent?

   a) The notary public's email address.
   b) The notary public's personal identification number.
   c) The signature of the person granting consent.
   d) The notary public's thumbprint.

120. In New York, a notarial certificate of consent commonly uses.

   a) Financial transactions.
   b) Real estate transactions.
   c) Family law matters.
   d) Employment contracts.

121. What should a Notary Public do when presented with an expired identification document?

   a) Refuse to notarize the document.
   b) Notarize the document and include a note about the expired identification.
   c) Extend the expiration date on the identification document.
   d) Verify the identity of the signer through alternative means.

122. A Notary Public can accept an identification document that expires within the last 30 days.

   a) True
   b) False

123. When a document lacks required elements, what should a Notary Public do?

   a) Refuse to notarize the document.
   b) Create a separate affidavit to provide the missing information.
   c) Complete the missing elements on behalf of the signer.
   d) Notarize the document and inform the signer of the missing elements.

124. What action should a Notary Public take when presented with a document that contains blank spaces?

   a) Notarize the document and leave the blank spaces as is.
   b) Complete the blank spaces on behalf of the signer.
   c) Refuse to notarize the document until the blank spaces fill.
   d) Notarize the document and include a note about the blank spaces.

125. A Notary Public can rely on their judgment to determine the validity of a document.

  a) True

  b) False

126. What should a Notary Public do when presented with a document that appears fraudulent or altered?

  a) Notarize the document and notify the appropriate authorities.

  b) Contact the signer's attorney for guidance.

  c) Refuse to notarize the document and report the suspicious activity.

  d) Consult with other Notary Publics for a consensus.

127. How should a Notary Public handle a document executed in a different state or country?

  a) Notarize the document as long as the signer has a valid identification.

  b) Contact the appropriate authorities in the executing state or country.

  c) Refuse to notarize the document due to jurisdictional limitations.

  d) Notarize the document and include a note about the different jurisdictions.

128. A Notary Public can correct errors or omissions on a completed document.

  a) True

  b) False

129. What should a Notary Public do if a document writes in a language they do not understand?

  a) Notarize the document and rely on a translation app for comprehension.

  b) Decline to notarize the document and recommend finding a qualified translator.

  c) Sign the document as a witness and provide an affidavit of understanding.

  d) Request the signer to provide a translation of the document.

130. What action should a Notary Public take if the notarial certificate is missing from a document?

  a) Refuse to notarize the document.

  b) Create a new notarial certificate and attach it to the document.

  c) Stamp their notary seal directly on the document.

  d) Sign the document and include a note about the missing notarial certificate.

131. A Notary Public may certify a copy of an expired identification document.

  a) True

  b) False

132. What should a Notary Public do if the document lacks the required signatures?

a) Notarize the document and include a note about the missing signatures.
b) Refuse to notarize the document until the missing signatures provide.
c) Sign the document as a witness and provide an affidavit of missing signatures.
d) Stamp their notary seal on the document in place of the missing signatures.

133. When a document contains contradictory information, what should a Notary Public do?

a) Notarize the document based on their interpretation.
b) Request clarification from the signer or the document's creator.
c) Complete the document according to their understanding of the signer's intent.
d) Refuse to notarize the document and recommend seeking legal advice.

134. A Notary Public can correct a mistake on a completed notarial certificate.

a) True
b) False

135. How should a Notary Public handle a document signed by a deceased person?

a) Notarize the document and note the date of the signer's passing.
b) Decline to notarize the document and inform the signer's family.
c) Sign the document as a witness and provide an affidavit of the signer's passing.
d) Refuse to notarize the document and recommend consulting an attorney.

136. What should a Notary Public do if they suspect the signer lacks the mental capacity to understand the document?

a) Notarize the document and assume the signer understands its contents.
b) Request a medical evaluation to determine the signer's mental capacity.
c) Refuse to notarize the document and recommend seeking legal advice.
d) Sign the document as a witness and provide an affidavit of the signer's mental capacity.

137. A Notary Public can notarize a document executed by a person with a power of attorney.

a) True
b) False

138. What should a Notary Public do if the document lacks a required notarial act?

a) Notarize the document and perform the missing notarial act.
b) Refuse to notarize the document until the missing notarial act provides.
c) Sign the document as a witness and provide an affidavit of the missing notarial act.
d) Stamp their notary seal on the document to fulfill the missing notarial act.

139. How should a Notary Public handle a document missing the necessary attachments or exhibits?

a) Notarize the document and note the missing attachments or exhibits.

b) Attach blank pages in place of the missing attachments or exhibits.

c) Refuse to notarize the document until the missing attachments or exhibits provide.

d) Stamp their notary seal directly on the document to indicate the missing attachments or exhibits.

140. A Notary Public can notarize a document executed by someone who cannot sign.

a) True

b) False

141. What should a Notary Public do if they receive conflicting instructions regarding the notarization from multiple parties?

a) Notarize the document based on their judgment.

b) Decline to notarize the document and recommend resolving the conflict.

c) Sign the document as a witness and provide an affidavit of the conflicting instructions.

d) Notarize the document and include a note about the conflicting instructions.

142. What should a Notary Public do when a document is incomplete or partially filled?

a) Complete the document on behalf of the signer.

b) Refuse to notarize the document until it is complete.

c) Sign the document as a witness and provide an affidavit of the incomplete sections.

d) Notarize the document and include a note about the incomplete sections.

143. A Notary Public can notarize a document executed by someone who does not understand the document's language.

a) True

b) False

144. What action should a Notary Public take if a document contains outdated or incorrect information?

a) Notarize the document and include a note about the outdated or incorrect information.

b) Correct the information on behalf of the signer to ensure accuracy.

c) Refuse to notarize the document until the outdated or incorrect information is corrected.

d) Sign the document as a witness and provide an affidavit of the outdated or incorrect information.

145. How should a Notary Public handle a document missing the required notarial certificate of acknowledgment or jurat?

a) Notarize the document and create a separate notarial certificate to attach.
b) Refuse to notarize the document until the missing notarial certificate provides.
c) Sign the document as a witness and provide an affidavit of the missing notarial certificate.
d) Stamp their notary seal on the document to serve as the missing notarial certificate.

146. A Notary Public can notarize a document executed by someone who refuses to provide identification.

a) True
b) False

147. What should a Notary Public do if a document contains conflicting information about the signer's identity?

a) Notarize the document and include a note about the conflicting information.
b) Contact the signer's employer or reference for verification.
c) Refuse to notarize the document and request clarification from the signer.
d) Sign the document as a witness and provide an affidavit of the conflicting information.

148. How should a Notary Public handle a document that is illegible or contains indecipherable markings?

a) Notarize the document and note the illegible or indecipherable markings.
b) Attempt to interpret the markings to the best of their ability.
c) Refuse to notarize the document until it is readable and clear.
d) Sign the document as a witness and provide an affidavit of the illegible or indecipherable markings.

149. A Notary Public can notarize a document executed by a person who is not physically present.

a) True
b) False

150. What should a Notary Public do if a document contains contradictory or conflicting notarial certificates?

a) Notarize the document based on their judgment.
b) Contact the issuing authority for clarification.
c) Refuse to notarize the document and recommend resolving the conflict.
d) Sign the document as a witness and provide an affidavit of the conflicting notarial certificates.

151. What is a conflict of interest for a Notary Public?

    a) A situation where the Notary Public has a personal or financial interest in the transaction or document notarized.

    b) A situation where the Notary Public is related to the signer by marriage.

    c) A situation where the Notary Public is not familiar with the language of the document notarized.

    d) A situation where the Notary Public has previously notarized documents for the same individual.

152. Notaries Public can notarize documents for family members and close friends without disclosing the relationship.

    a) True

    b) False

153. What should a Notary Public do if they have a personal or financial interest in a document to be notarized?

    a) Disclose the conflict of interest and refuse to notarize the document.

    b) Notarize the document and disclose the conflict of interest in the notarial certificate.

    c) Transfer the notarial duties to another Notary Public.

    d) Notarize the document without disclosing the conflict of interest.

154. A Notary Public can notarize a document for a business in which they hold a financial stake.

    a) True

    b) False

155. When should a Notary Public disclose a conflict of interest?

    a) Only if the signer specifically asks about potential conflicts.

    b) In all situations where a conflict of interest exists.

    c) Only if the conflict of interest may result in financial gain.

    d) When the document notarized involves real estate transactions.

156. A Notary Public can notarize a document for their employer if they hold a managerial position.

    a) True

    b) False

157. What should a Notary Public do if they inadvertently notarize a document with a conflict of interest?

    a) Notify the appropriate authorities and report the incident.

b) Take no action, as the notarization is already complete.

c) Inform the signer of the conflict of interest after the notarization.

d) Contact an attorney for legal advice.

158. A Notary Public can notarize a document for a business partner.

a) True

b) False

159. What should a Notary Public do if uncertain whether a conflict of interest exists?

a) Proceed with the notarization to avoid delaying the transaction.

b) Consult with a colleague or mentor for guidance.

c) Disclose the potential conflict of interest to the signer for their decision.

d) Refuse to notarize the document until the conflict of interest resolves.

160. A Notary Public can notarize a document for immediate family members.

a) True

b) False

161. How should a Notary Public handle a situation where they are notarizing a document for a close friend?

a) Proceed with the notarization without disclosing the relationship.

b) Disclose the relationship and obtain written consent from the friend.

c) Refuse to notarize the document due to the conflict of interest.

d) Seek legal advice before proceeding with the notarization.

162. A Notary Public can notarize a document for a business competitor.

a) True

b) False

163. What should a Notary Public do if a client offers a gift or gratuity in exchange for notarizing a document?

a) Accept the gift as a token of appreciation for their services.

b) Decline the gift and continue with the notarization.

c) Report the incident to the appropriate authorities.

d) Return the gift and refuse to notarize the document.

164. A Notary Public can notarize a document for a close relative if they are not personally involved in the transaction.

a) True

b) False

165. What should a Notary Public do if they have a financial interest in the property notarized in a real estate transaction?

    a) Disclose the conflict of interest and refuse to notarize the document.

    b) Notarize the document and include a note about the financial interest.

    c) Transfer the notarial duties to another Notary Public.

    d) Consult with an attorney before proceeding with the notarization.

166. A Notary Public can notarize a document for a client if they have a personal relationship with the client's attorney.

    a) True

    b) False

167. What action should a Notary Public take if they become aware of a conflict of interest after the notarization is complete?

    a) Contact the signer and inform them of the conflict of interest.

    b) Notify the appropriate authorities and seek legal advice.

    c) Keep the information confidential to avoid legal implications.

    d) Retract the notarization and refund any fees collected.

168. A Notary Public can notarize a document for their landlord or tenant.

    a) True

    b) False

    Answer: b) False

169. How should a Notary Public handle a situation where they have a financial interest in a business that is a party to the document notarized?

    a) Disclose the conflict of interest and offer to recuse themselves from the notarization.

    b) Proceed with the notarization and disclose the conflict of interest in the notarial certificate.

    c) Transfer the notarial duties to another Notary Public.

    d) Seek legal advice before deciding how to proceed.

170. A Notary Public can notarize a document for their employer's clients.

    a) True

    b) False

171. What should a Notary Public do if they have a personal relationship with the person requesting the notarization but have no financial interest in the transaction?

    a) Proceed with the notarization but disclose the personal relationship.

    b) Transfer the notarial duties to another Notary Public.

    c) Refuse to notarize the document due to the conflict of interest.

    d) Seek legal advice before deciding how to proceed.

172. A Notary Public can notarize a document for a client if they have previously provided legal advice to the client.

    a) True

    b) False

173. What should a Notary Public do if they have a personal interest in a document but are not a party to the transaction?

    a) Disclose the personal interest and obtain all parties' written consent.

    b) Notarize the document and include a note about the personal interest.

    c) Refuse to notarize the document due to the conflict of interest.

    d) Consult with an attorney before deciding how to proceed.

174. A Notary Public can notarize a document for a business entity in which they hold stock.

    a) True

    b) False

175. What should a Notary Public do if they have a personal relationship with the signer but no financial interest in the document?

    a) Proceed with the notarization and disclose the personal relationship.

    b) Refuse to notarize the document due to the conflict of interest.

    c) Transfer the notarial duties to another Notary Public.

    d) Consult with an attorney before deciding how to proceed.

176. A Notary Public can notarize a document for a client if they have a personal relationship with the client's accountant.

    a) True

    b) False

177. What should a Notary Public do if they have a financial interest in a document but are not a party to the transaction?

    a) Disclose the financial interest and obtain all parties' written consent.

    b) Refuse to notarize the document due to the conflict of interest.

    c) Notarize the document and include a note about the financial interest.

    d) Seek legal advice before deciding how to proceed.

178. A Notary Public can notarize a document for their co-worker.

    a) True

b) False

179. What should a Notary Public do if they notarize a document for a friend but do not have a personal or financial interest in the transaction?

a) Proceed with the notarization and disclose the friendship.
b) Transfer the notarial duties to another Notary Public.
c) Refuse to notarize the document due to the conflict of interest.
d) Seek legal advice before deciding how to proceed.

180. A Notary Public can notarize a document for a client if they have a personal relationship with the client's insurance agent.

a) True
b) False

181. Which of the following documents typically require an oath or affirmation by a notary public?

a) Power of Attorney
b) Birth Certificate
c) Marriage License
d) Rental Agreement

182. What is the purpose of administering an oath or affirmation?

a) To verify the identity of the document signer
b) To ensure the document is legally binding
c) To deter fraud or false statements
d) To authorize the notary public's stamp

183. When administering an oath, the notary public should:

a) Make sure the document signer understands the oath,
b) Read the entire document aloud,
c) Ask for identification from the document signer,
d) Sign the document as a witness

184. Which of the following statements is accurate regarding administering an oath?

a) The notary public must write the oath on a separate sheet of paper.
b) The document signer must place their hand on a Bible.
c) The document signer must repeat the entire document word-for-word.
d) The notary public should ask the document signer to raise their right hand.

185. Can a notary public administer an oath to themselves?

a) Yes, as long as it is for their document.

b) No, a notary public cannot administer an oath to themselves.

c) Yes, if they have no other option available.

d) Yes, as long as it is for a family member.

186. Which of the following statements is true regarding certification by a notary public?

a) Certification can do for legal documents.

b) Certification verifies the accuracy of a document copy.

c) Certification requires the presence of a witness.

d) Certification is optional for notary publics.

187. When certifying a document copy, a notary public should:

a) Make a photocopy of the original document.

b) Compare the copy to the original document.

c) Sign and stamp the original document.

d) Witness the document signer's signature.

188. Which documents can a notary public certify as a true copy?

a) Driver's license

b) Social Security card

c) Birth certificate

d) All of the above

189. Can a notary public certify an electronic document?

a) Yes, by electronically signing and stamping the document.

b) No, certification can do for physical copies.

c) Yes, but only if the document is printed and notarized in person.

d) Yes, but only if the document is password-protected.

190. How should a notary public sign and seal a certified document?

a) With their official stamp and signature

b) With their initials and date

c) With a blue ink pen and printed name

d) With the document signer's signature

191. Can a notary public certify a translation of a document?

a) Yes, as long as they are fluent in both languages.

b) No, translation certification requires a separate translator.

c) Yes, but only if the document is notarized in the original language.

    d) Yes, as long as the notary public does the translation.

192. Which of the following is an example of an oath a notary public can administer?

    a) "I swear to tell the truth, the whole truth, and nothing but the truth."

    b) "I certify that the information in this document is true and correct."

    c) "I acknowledge my signature on this document."

    d) "I promise to repay the loan according to the policy. "

193. When administering an oath, can a notary public alter the wording of the oath?

    a) Yes, as long as it conveys the same meaning.

    b) the oath's wording must be as the law prescribes.

    c) Yes, as long as the document signer agrees to the changes.

    d) No, an attorney can only change the oath's wording.

194. How many witnesses require for an oath?

    a) One

    b) Two

    c) Three

    d) None

195. Can a notary public administer an oath over video conference (e.g., Zoom)?

    a) Yes, as long as the document signer is physically present in New York.

    b) Yes, but only if the notary public is an attorney.

    c) No, the document signer must be physically present with the notary public.

    d) No, video conferencing is not allowed for oath administration.

196. Which of the following is NOT a requirement for a notary public to administer an oath?

    a) The document signer's consent to the oath.

    b) The document sign must notarize.

    c) The state of New York must commission the notary public.

    d) The notary public must administer the oath in person.

197. When certifying a document copy, a notary public must:

    a) Make a note on the copy indicating it is a certified true copy.

    b) Write a statement on the copy explaining the purpose of the certification.

    c) Include their notary public commission expiration date on the copy.

    d) None of the above.

198. Can a notary public certify a document that is already notarized?

    a) Yes, but only if the original notary public is unavailable.

b) Certification is optional for already notarized documents.

c) Yes, as long as the document signer requests it.

d) No, a document cannot notarize more than once.

199. Which of the following statements is true regarding certification by a notary public?

a) Certification guarantees the accuracy of the document contents.

b) Certification is only valid for a limited period.

c) Certification requires the document signer to take an oath.

d) Certification can only do for government-issued documents.

200. Can a notary public certify a document written in a language they do not understand?

a) Yes, as long as they can verify the document's authenticity.

b) No, a notary public must understand the document they certify.

c) Yes, as long as a translator is present during the certification.

d) No, certification is not available for documents written in foreign languages.

201. What is the primary purpose of administering an oath in the notarial process?

a) To ensure the document's legality

b) To confirm the signer's identity

c) To deter fraudulent behavior

d) To authorize the notary's actions

202. How should a notary public sign their name on a certified document copy?

a) By printing their name

b) By signing as a witness

c) By using their official stamp

d) By using their official signature

203. When certifying a document copy, the notary public should:

a) Place a special seal on the document

b) Date and sign the document

c) Attach a notarial certificate to the document

d) All of the above

204. Can a notary public charge a fee for administering an oath or certification?

a) Yes, but only for administering an oath

b) Yes, but only for certification of documents

c) Yes, for both administering an oath and certification of documents

d) No, notaries public cannot charge fees for these services

205. How should a notary public correct a mistake in a certified document copy?

a) Cross out the mistake and initial it
b) Use correction fluid to cover the mistake
c) Start over with a new document copy
d) None

206. Which of the following documents typically requires a notary public's certification?

a) last will
b) Passport Application
c) Employment Contract
d) Vehicle Registration

207. What should a notary public do if a document signer refuses to take an oath?

a) Refuse to notarize the document
b) Administer the oath without the signer's consent
c) Proceed with notarization without administering an oath
d) Call the police to handle the situation

208. Can a notary public certify a document copy that contains confidential information?

a) Yes, as long as the document signer consents to the certification.
b) No, a notary public should not certify confidential documents.
c) Yes, but only if the confidential information is redacted.
d) Yes, as long as the document copy is stored securely.

209. How should a notary public handle a situation where the document signer cannot physically raise their right hand for an oath?

a) They can use the left hand instead.
b) They should proceed with the oath regardless of hand-raising.
c) They should consult a legal expert for guidance.
d) They should use an alternative method to affirm the oath.

210. Can a notary public certify a document if the original is not available?

a) Yes, as long as a valid copy is present.
b) No, a notary public can only certify original documents.
c) Yes, but only if the document signer provides an affidavit.
d) No, certification requires the inspection of the original document.

211. What is the primary purpose of document management techniques in notary practice?

a) Enhancing document aesthetics
b) Ensuring document confidentiality

c) Facilitating document delivery

d) Minimizing document storage costs

212. Which of the following is a recommended practice for document storage in a notary office?

a) Keeping documents in an unlocked filing cabinet

b) Storing documents in a public storage facility

c) Using a secure, locked filing system

d) Digitally storing documents on a shared server

213. How long should a notary typically retain a copy of a notarized document?

a) six months

b) 1 year

c) 3 years

d) 5 years

214. Which of the following is essential when handling sensitive or confidential documents?

a) Sharing them freely with colleagues

b) Leaving them unattended in public areas,

c) Encrypting them when transmitting

d) Electronically. Discarding them in regular waste bins

215. Which of the following is a secure method of document disposal?

a) Tearing the documents into small pieces by hand

b) Burning the documents in an open fire

c) Recycling the documents without shredding

d) Shredding the documents using a cross-cut shredder

216. When making a backup of digital documents, what should a notary consider?

a) Using a USB flash drive for backup

b) Storing the backup in an unsecured cloud storage service

c) Encrypting the backup to protect sensitive information

d) Making backups only once a year to save time

217. What is the purpose of implementing version control for notary documents?

a) To track changes made to records over time

b) To limit access to records by unauthorized individuals

c) To ensure all documents are in the same format,

d) To generate automated summaries of document content

218. Which of the following is an essential feature of a secure document management system?

- a) Public access to all documents
- b) single-factor authentication for users
- c) Regular system backups and disaster recovery plan
- d) An open-source platform with community support

219. What does the term "metadata" refer to in document management?

- a) The physical characteristics of a document, such as paper type and ink color
- b) The content and structure of document
- c) Information about a record, such as an author, creation date, and file size,
- d) The procedure of converting physical documents into digital format

220. What is the recommended approach for organizing and labeling physical documents?

- a) Using an arbitrary naming system for easy identification
- b) Storing documents in random order for quick access
- c) Grouping documents by date, category, or client name.
- d) Keeping all records in a single folder to save space

221. What should a notary do if a document is damaged or altered before notarization?

- a) Proceed with the notarization as long as the content is still legible
- b) Reject the paper and request a new, undamaged copy
- c) Notify the client and seek legal advice on how to proceed
- d) Alter the document back to its original state and proceed with notarization

222. Which of the following is a potential risk of sharing digital documents via email?

- a) Limited accessibility for recipients
- b) Increased risk of unauthorized access or interception
- c) Difficulty in attaching large files to emails
- d) Loss of document formatting during transmission

223. How should a notary protect physical documents when transporting them off-site?

- a) Place them in a personal bag or purse
- b) Leave them unattended in a locked vehicle
- c) Use a secure bag or briefcase designed for document transport
- d) Carry them openly in hand to prevent theft

224. What is the role of access controls in document management?

- a) Restricting access to only authorized individuals
- b) Ensuring all documents print in color
- c) Allowing public access to all documents for transparency

d) Automatically convert documents to PDF format

225. Which of the following is a recommended practice for preventing document loss?

a) Keeping backup copies in an unlocked drawer
b) Storing documents in multiple physical locations
c) Sharing documents via unencrypted USB drives
d) Ignoring regular backups to save time and storage space

226. What is the purpose of implementing a document retention policy?

a) To ensure documents are destroyed immediately after notarization
b) To establish guidelines for document storage and retention
c) To limit the number of copies a notary can handle,
d) To prevent documents from being stored in electronic format

227. How should a notary handle original documents provided by clients?

a) Keep them secure and return them promptly after notarization
b) Retain them indefinitely as a record of the notarial act
c) Dispose of them immediately after notarization
d) Share them freely with colleagues for reference

228. Which of the following is an example of a digital document format commonly used in notary practice?

a) PDF (Portable Document Format)
b) MP3 (MPEG Audio Layer 3)
c) XLS (Microsoft Excel Spreadsheet)
d) JPG (Joint Photographic Experts Group)

229. How should a notary protect digital documents from unauthorized access?

a) Use weak passwords for digital document storage
b) Share documents via public file-sharing platforms
c) Implement strong passwords and access controls
d) Store documents in unencrypted folders on local drives

230. Which of the following is an example of a cloud-based document management system?

a) Local network server
b) External hard drive
c) Dropbox
d) USB flash drive

231. How can a notary ensure the integrity of electronic documents?

a) By converting them to physical copies
b) By regularly printing and signing digital documents,
c) By implementing digital signatures or electronic seals,
d) By avoiding the use of electronic records altogether

232. What should a notary do if they suspect a document has been tampered with?

a) Proceed with the notarization as long as the content remains unchanged
b) Reject the record and notify the relevant authorities
c) Alter the composition back to its original state before notarization
d) Consult a colleague for advice on how to proceed

233. How should a notary handle document revisions or amendments?

a) Remove all previous versions from storage
b) Keep a record of all versions and revisions
c) Ignore modifications and proceed with notarization as planned initially.
d) Share revised documents without notifying relevant parties.

234. What should a notary do if they accidentally notarize the wrong document?

a) Alter the notarial certificate to match the correct document
b) Tear up the notarial certificate and start the notarization process again
c) Notify all parties involved and rectify the mistake promptly
d) Ignore the error and proceed with the original notarization

235. Which of the following is an example of a document management best practice?

a) Mixing original and copy documents
b) storing documents in damp or humid areas
c) regularly reviewing and purging outdated documents
d) Using low-quality paper for document printing

236. What is the purpose of implementing a disaster recovery plan for document management?

a) To ensure all documents destroy in case of a disaster
b) To establish protocols for document restoration after a disaster
c) To avoid backing up documents in multiple locations,
d) To create additional physical copies of documents for redundancy

237. What should a notary do if they receive a document with missing or incomplete information?

a) Proceed with notarization and assume the missing information is accurate

b) Refrain from notarizing the paper until all necessary information is provided

c) Fill in the missing data themselves without consulting the client

d) Ask the client to give additional documents to compensate for the missing information

238. How should a notary handle physical documents that are no longer needed?

a) Discard them in regular waste bins

b) Store them indefinitely for reference

c) Shred them using a cross-cut shredder

d) Donate them to a local library or charity

239. What is the purpose of document indexing in a notary office?

a) To create an organized and searchable database of documents

b) To generate automatic summaries of document content

c) To establish document ownership and copyright information

d) To ensure all copies print in a consistent font and size,

240. How should a notary handle documents that contain personally identifiable information (PII)?

a) Share them freely with colleagues for collaboration

b) Encrypt them before transmitting or storing them digitally

c) Print and keep them without any additional security measures

d) Store them in an unlocked drawer for easy access

241. Which of the following is not a permissible fee for a Notary Public in New York?

a) Fee for administering an oath or affirmation

b) Fee for taking an acknowledgment

c) Fee for notarizing a document

d) Fee for providing legal advice

242. What is the responsibility of a Notary Public regarding collecting and storing personal information?

a) Notary Publics are not allowed to collect personal information

b) Notary Publics must securely store personal information

c) Notary Publics must share personal information with government agencies

d) Notary Publics must publicly disclose personal information

243. Can a Notary Public disclose personal information obtained during notarization to third parties without the client's consent?

a) Yes, but only if required by law

b) Yes, without any restrictions

c) No, personal information must not disclose without consent

d) Only if approved by the Secretary of State.

244. How long should a Notary Public retain personal information collected during notarization?

a) 1 year

b) 3 years

c) 5 years

d) 7 years

245. Can a Notary Public store personal information electronically?

a) Yes, but only if encrypted and password-protected

b) Yes, without any restrictions

c) No, personal information must be stored in physical formats

d) Only if approved by the client

246. What steps should a Notary Public take to dispose of personal information securely?

a) Shredding or permanently deleting the information

b) Handing over the information to the client

c) Selling the information to data brokers

d) Sharing the information on social media

247. Can a Notary Public use personal information obtained during notarization for marketing purposes?

a) Yes, with the client's consent

b) Yes, without any restrictions

c) No, personal information cannot uses for marketing purposes

d) Only if approved by the Secretary of State

248. Can a Notary Public request additional personal information from the client beyond what is necessary for notarization?

a) Yes, with the client's consent

b) Yes, without any restrictions

c) No, additional personal information should not request

d) Only if approved by the Secretary of State

249. What should a Notary Public do if there is a suspected data breach or unauthorized access to personal information?

a) Immediately notify the affected individuals and appropriate authorities

b) Ignore the incident and continue notarization services

c) Delete all personal information to prevent further breaches

d) Only if approved by the Secretary of State

250. How should a Notary Public handle physical documents containing personal information after notarization?

a) Store them in a locked cabinet or secure location

b) Discard them in regular trash bins

c) Donate them to local libraries

d) Keep them accessible to the public

Chapter 6

Practice Test - Answers

1. **Answer: b) To witness and authenticate signatures**

Explanation: The primary role of a Notary Public is to witness and authenticate signatures on legal documents. Notaries are impartial witnesses who verify the identity of the signatories and ensure the documents' authenticity. They do not provide legal advice or represent clients in court; rather, their duty is to certify the validity of signatures, thereby enhancing the documents' credibility and legality.

2. **Answer: c) State jurisdiction**

Explanation: A Notary Public operates within the jurisdiction of the state in which they are commissioned. Each state has its own laws and regulations governing notarial acts. Therefore, the authority of a Notary Public is limited to the boundaries of the state where they are licensed to practice. They cannot perform notarial acts outside their designated state jurisdiction.

3. **Answer: c) To provide notarial services**

Explanation: The purpose of a Notary Public's jurisdiction is to provide notarial services, which include witnessing signatures, administering oaths, and certifying documents. Notaries play a vital role in ensuring the authenticity and integrity of legal documents within their designated jurisdiction. While they may be involved in legal proceedings tangentially by notarizing documents related to criminal cases or civil lawsuits, their primary function is to facilitate proper documentation and maintain legal standards.

4. **Answer: a) United States**

Explanation: A Notary Public's jurisdiction lies within the country where they are commissioned. In this case, it is the United States. Notaries are authorized to perform their duties within the boundaries of the state in which they are licensed.

5. Answer: c) Yes, under certain conditions

Explanation: Notaries may authenticate signatures outside their jurisdiction under specific circumstances, such as when the document being signed is related to a matter governed by the laws of the notary's home state, or when allowed by the laws of the state where the notary is acting.

6. Answer: c) Witnessing the signing of documents

Explanation: One of the primary responsibilities of a Notary Public is to witness the signing of documents and verify the identity of the signatories. Notaries do not provide legal advice, make court judgments, or draft legal contracts; their role is focused on ensuring the authenticity and legality of signatures and documents.

7. Answer: b) No, never

Explanation: A Notary Public is not responsible for determining the validity of a document's content. Their role primarily involves verifying the identity of signers and ensuring the proper execution of the document in accordance with legal requirements. Determining the content's validity falls under the purview of legal professionals or relevant authorities.

8. Answer: c) Yes, in certain situations

Explanation: A Notary Public can refuse to provide services if there are conflicts of interest, especially when such conflicts may compromise the impartiality and integrity of the notarization process. Upholding ethical standards and avoiding conflicts of interest are essential aspects of a Notary Public's responsibilities.

9. Answer: d) Signatures on legal documents

Explanation: Notary Publics authenticate signatures on legal documents by verifying the identity of signers and ensuring they are signing willingly and knowingly. While they may handle various documents in their capacity, their primary function revolves around verifying signatures and administering oaths, affirmations, or acknowledgments.

10. Answer: c) To authenticate the Notary Public's signature

Explanation: The primary purpose of a Notary Public's seal or stamp is to authenticate the Notary Public's signature, indicating that the document has been properly notarized.

11. Answer: c) Yes, in certain situations

Explanation: While generally, a Notary Public must witness the signing of a document, there are exceptions where remote notarization or other procedures may be permitted depending on the jurisdiction and circumstances.

12. Answer: b) State government

Explanation: The authority to appoint Notaries Public is typically granted by the state government. Each state has its own laws and regulations governing the qualifications and duties of

Notaries Public.

13. Answer: d) No, only attorneys can do so

Explanation: Notary Publics are not authorized to provide legal advice or services; this is the role of licensed attorneys. Notaries simply witness the signing of documents and verify the identity of the signers.

14. Answer: c) 4 years

Explanation: While the term of office for a Notary Public can vary by state, in most states, a Notary Public serves a term of four years.

15. Answer: c) Yes, within certain limits set by law

Explanation: Notary Publics can charge fees for their services, but these fees are typically capped at a maximum amount as set by law. The exact fee limits can vary from state to state.

16. Answer: b) No, never

Explanation: A Notary Public must be able to understand the document in order to ensure the integrity of the notarization process. If the notary cannot understand the document, they cannot be certain that the document is complete and that the signers are aware of the contents. A translator's presence does not change this requirement.

17. Answer: c) Yes, within certain limits set by law

Explanation: A Notary Public is typically required by law to maintain a record book or journal of their notarial acts. However, the specific requirements, including what details must be recorded and how long the records must be kept, can vary by jurisdiction.

18. Answer: b) No, never

Explanation: A Notary Public cannot notarize their own signature as it presents a conflict of interest and undermines the integrity of the notarization. The role of a Notary is to serve as an impartial witness.

19. Answer: a) Yes, always

Explanation: A Notary Public has the authority to refuse to notarize a document with blank spaces to prevent fraud or potential alterations after the notarization.

20. Answer: b) No, never

Explanation: A Notary Public's role is to verify the identity of the signatories and the authenticity of signatures, not the accuracy of the information contained within the document.

21. Answer: c) Yes, in certain situations

Explanation: A Notary Public may provide services to family members unless it involves a document in which the Notary or a family member has a financial or beneficial interest. The specific rules about notarizing for family members can vary by state.

22. Answer: a) Yes, always

Explanation: A Notary Public is authorized to refuse to notarize a document if the signatory appears to be under the influence of drugs or alcohol, which may impair their ability to understand the nature of the transaction.

23. Answer: a) Yes, always

Explanation: A Notary Public must always secure their official seal or stamp to prevent misuse or fraud. This is a fundamental responsibility to ensure that the notary's credentials are not used without their authorization.

24. Answer: c) Yes, in certain situations

Explanation: Notaries can certify copies of certain documents, but not all. For instance, public records or court documents typically cannot be certified by a notary. The notary must follow the guidelines set by their jurisdiction.

25. Answer: a) Yes, always

Explanation: If a signatory does not understand the content of a document, a Notary Public must refuse to notarize. This ensures that signatories are aware of and understand what they are signing, which is crucial for the document's legal effectiveness.

26. Answer: b) No, never

Explanation: Notarizing a spouse's signature is generally not allowed as it presents a conflict of interest and can call into question the impartiality of the notarization.

27. Answer: c) Yes, within certain limits set by law

Explanation: If the signatory does not have traditional forms of identification, a Notary Public may be able to use alternative methods such as a credible witness, depending on the laws of the jurisdiction.

28. Answer: b) No, never

Explanation: Notaries are commissioned by their home state and can only provide notarial services within that state unless they have a commission in the state where they are performing the notarial act.

29. Answer: b) No, never

Explanation: A Notary Public must not notarize a document if they have a personal interest in the transaction to maintain their role as an impartial witness.

30. Answer: d) Driver's license

Explanation: A driver's license is a commonly accepted form of identification for notarization as it is government-issued, contains a photo, and typically includes a signature for comparison.

31. Answer: b) Compare the signature on the identification document with the signature on the notarized document

Explanation: The Notary Public must verify the identity of the signatory by comparing the signature on the presented identification with the signature on the document to be notarized, ensuring they match to confirm the identity of the signatory.

32. Answer: b) False

Explanation: In New York, a Notary Public can notarize based on personal knowledge of the signatory, but it is not a practice solely relied upon without any identification documents.

33. d) Accept a witness statement from another individual

Explanation: In lieu of valid identification, a Notary Public in New York may rely on the sworn statement of a witness who knows the signatory and who presents valid ID themselves.

34. Answer: d) Utility bill

Explanation: A utility bill is generally not considered an acceptable form of identification for notarial purposes because it does not include a photo or signature of the holder.

35. Answer: a) The signatory provides an expired identification document

Explanation: A Notary Public should not notarize if the presented identification document is expired as it does not satisfy the requirement for a valid form of ID.

36. Answer: b) False

Explanation: New York does not have a statutory requirement for Notaries to keep a journal of their notarial acts, including recording the IDs of signatories, although it is recommended best practice.

37. Answer: a) not legally required to keep a record book or journal of notarial acts

Explanation: In New York, Notary Publics are not legally required to keep a record book or journal of notarial acts, including records of identification presented by a signatory. However, the New York Department of State Division of Licensing Services and the Notary Public License Law recommend as a best practice that Notaries maintain a record book for at least 10 years to protect themselves. This record book should include significant details about the notarizations they perform, but they are not mandated to record the type of identification presented by a signatory. If a New York Notary Public opts to record such details voluntarily, retaining these records for the duration of their commission or for the suggested 10 years could provide a helpful reference in case any notarization is questioned in the future.

38. Answer: c) The type of identification presented

Explanation: While New York does not require a record book, if a Notary Public chooses to maintain one, it should include pertinent information such as the type of identification presented.

39. Answer: a) The signatory is unable to provide a valid identification document

Explanation: If a signatory cannot provide a valid form of identification, the Notary Public must refuse to notarize to ensure the integrity of the notarization process.

40. Answer: b) Foreign passport

Explanation: A foreign passport is an acceptable form of identification for non-U.S. citizens in New York, as it is government-issued, includes a photo, and is normally stamped by the Department of Homeland Security.

41. Answer: b) False

Explanation: Notaries in New York cannot rely on expired identification documents to establish a signatory's identity.

42. Answer: b) Accept a mark or signature made by a witness on behalf of the signatory

Explanation: If a signatory is physically unable to sign, a Notary Public can accept a signature or mark made by a witness at the direction of the signatory, and the witness must also sign their name. The Notary should note the circumstances in their journal if they maintain one.

43. Answer: d) The signatory's identification document appears altered or forged

Explanation: A Notary Public must refuse to notarize if the identification document presented appears to be altered or forged as it compromises the integrity of the notarization.

44. Answer: c) Both the front and back sides of the identification document

Explanation: A Notary Public must examine both the front and back sides of an identification document to verify its authenticity and to check for any signs of tampering or fraud.

45. Answer: b) False

Explanation: A Notary Public cannot use their own personal identification documents to verify the identity of a signatory. They must rely on the identification presented by the signatory themselves.

46. Answer: c) Library card

Explanation: Library cards are generally not accepted as valid identification for notarization because they do not meet the standard criteria for identification, such as having a photo, signature, and security features.

47. Answer: c) Request an additional form of identification from the signatory

Explanation: If a Notary Public suspects that an identification document is fraudulent, they should request an additional form of identification and, if still uncertain, refuse to perform the notarization.

48. Answer: b) False

Explanation: A New York Notary Public is only authorized to notarize within the geographical boundaries of the state of New York.

49. Answer: a) Conduct an online search for the document's format and security features

Explanation: While a Notary Public can perform an online search to better understand a foreign identification document's format and security features, they should also use their best judgment and, if uncertain, refuse to notarize.

50. Answer: d) None of the above

Explanation: As none of the options listed are standard forms of identification, a Notary Public must rely on credible forms of identification with a photo and signature for a visually impaired signatory. If none are available, they should not perform the notarization.

51. Answer: b) False

Explanation: New York law does not require Notaries Public to keep a record book or journal of their notarial acts, though it is recommended as a best practice.

52. Answer: d) All of the above

Explanation: In New York, while it is not a requirement, including the signatory's identification information in the notarial certificate can be considered a best practice for acknowledgments, jurats, oaths, and affirmations to ensure thoroughness in the notarial act.

53. Answer: b) Refuse to notarize the document

Explanation: If an identification document lacks a photograph, which is a crucial component for verifying identity, the Notary Public should refuse to notarize the document, as New York State requires satisfactory evidence of the person's identity which typically includes a photograph.

54. Answer: b) False

Explanation: In New York, Notaries Public cannot accept expired identification documents. All identification must be current and valid at the time of notarization.

55. Answer: a) The signatory's identification document does not match the name on the document to be notarized

Explanation: A Notary Public must refuse to notarize if the name on the identification does not match the name on the document because this discrepancy calls into question the identity of the signatory.

56. Answer: c) Only accept the foreign passport if the U.S. Customs and Border Protection has stamped it

Explanation: A Notary Public in New York can accept a foreign passport as a valid form of identification if it has been stamped by the U.S. Customs and Border Protection, as this indicates the passport has been verified by a U.S. agency.

57. Answer: c) A neutral third party who knows both the signatory and the Notary Public

Explanation: A credible identifying witness should be a neutral third party who personally knows the individual whose document is being notarized and who is personally known to the Notary Public

58. Answer: b) False

Explanation: New York does not mandate formal training on identification procedures for Notary Publics. However, Notaries are expected to understand and properly execute the duties of their office, which includes verifying identities.

59. Answer: c) Refuse to notarize the document and report the suspicion to the appropriate authorities

Explanation: If a Notary Public suspects impersonation, they should refuse to notarize the document and may report their suspicion to appropriate authorities.

60. Answer: d) To notarize the document

Explanation: The purpose of authenticating a document by a Notary Public is to notarize it – to witness the signing and to verify the identity of the signatories, ensuring that the signatories are who they say they are.

61. Answer: c) Last will

Explanation: Last wills are among the types of documents that typically require notarization to attest to the authenticity of the signatures.

62. Answer: b) No, never

Explanation: Notaries Public should not notarize documents that contain blank spaces, as this could allow for fraudulent additions to the document after notarization.

63. Answer: b) To ensure its accuracy and completeness

Explanation: The Notary's role when authenticating a document is to ensure that the signatories' signatures are genuine and that the document is complete at the time of signing, not to determine the legal validity of the document's content.

64. Answer: c) Business invoices

Explanation: Business invoices are typically considered regular business records and do not generally require notarization. Documents like powers of attorney, contracts and agreements, and loan documents often require notarization because they are legal instruments.

65. Answer: c) Yes, with proper translation

Explanation: A Notary Public can notarize a document written in a foreign language if they can communicate with the signer and understand the type of notarial act required. However, the Notary Public must be able to understand what they are notarizing, either because they are familiar with the language or a reliable translation is available.

66. Answer: b) Notarization

Explanation: The process of a Notary Public authenticating a document is called notarization. This process involves verifying the identity of the signers, witnessing signatures, and marking documents with a seal or stamp to indicate the notarization.

67. Answer: c) Yes, under certain conditions

Explanation: A Notary Public can authenticate a copy of an original document only if state law allows it. Some states allow Notaries to make certified copies, while others do not.

68. Answer: c) Yes, under certain conditions

Explanation: A Notary Public can notarize a document signed electronically if their state laws permit electronic notarization and the Notary has the necessary technology and authorization to perform electronic notarizations.

69. Answer: d) All of the above

Explanation: When authenticating a document, the Notary Public should include the date and location of the notarization, their own contact information (which may include the Notary Public's name and commission details), and the signature of the document signer.

70. Answer: b) No, never

Explanation: A Notary Public must refuse to notarize if the signatory is mentally incapacitated or cannot understand the nature of the transaction, as this casts doubt on the signatory's ability to consent to the document.

71. c) Yes, under certain conditions

Explanation: Witnesses may be required to be present during notarization for certain documents or in certain states. The specific requirements depend on state law and the type of document being notarized.

72. Answer: b) No, never

Explanation: A Notary Public must not notarize an incomplete document or a document with missing information, as this could result in fraudulent additions to the document after notarization.

73. Answer: b) No, never

Explanation: It is incumbent upon a Notary Public to refuse to authenticate a document that exhibits any indication of alteration or tampering. Authenticating such a document would contravene notarial standards and potentially facilitate fraudulent activity.

74. Answer: c) Yes, under certain conditions

Explanation: A Notary Public may authenticate a document using a digital signature provided they comply with the relevant state laws pertaining to electronic notarization and possess the appropriate technology to do so.

75. Answer: c) Yes, under certain conditions

Explanation: The legibility of the handwriting on a document does not inherently preclude a Notary Public from performing authentication; however, the Notary must be able to sufficiently discern the document's content to ensure the act of notarization is executed properly.

76. Answer: c) Yes, under certain conditions

Explanation: A Notary Public can authenticate a document for a visually impaired signatory if the signatory can understand the document's nature and content, possibly through reading aloud or another accessible method.

77. Answer: b) No, never

Explanation: Notarization authenticates the identity of the signers and their signatures, not the content of the document. Therefore, if a document contains false information, the veracity of the content does not fall under the purview of a Notary Public.

78. Answer: c) Yes, under certain conditions

Explanation: Signatures made with a mark are recognized legally, provided the mark is intended as the signatory's signature and the notarization includes a witness to the signing.

79. Answer: b) No, never

Explanation: A Notary Public cannot authenticate a document that has expired or is otherwise invalid; the notarization would give the appearance of legal validity to an obsolete document.

80. Answer: b) No, never

Explanation: The physical presence of the signatory is a fundamental requirement for notarization. Absent the signatory's physical presence, the Notary Public must refuse to perform the notarial act.

81. Answer: c) Yes, under certain conditions

Explanation: A Notary Public may notarize a document for a minor if the minor presents acceptable identification and demonstrates an understanding of the transaction, although this may vary by state law.

82. Answer: c) Yes, under certain conditions

Explanation: If the signatory does not understand the language of the document, a Notary Public can proceed with notarization if it is clear that the signatory is aware of the document's significance and has willingly signed it.

83. Answer: b) No, never

Explanation: Notarization cannot proceed without the willing participation and signature of the signatory; compulsion or refusal to sign renders notarization null and void.

84. Answer: b) No, never

Explanation: If a signatory is under the influence of drugs or alcohol, they may lack the necessary capacity to understand the transaction, thereby obligating the Notary Public to decline notarization.

85. Answer: a) Yes, always

Explanation: The presence of a dispute over a document's content does not prevent a Notary Public from notarizing signatures. The role of the Notary is to verify signers' identities, not to adjudicate disputes.

86. Answer: c) Yes, under certain conditions

Explanation: Should a signatory be incapable of signing, alternative procedures may be followed, such as the use of a signature by mark, to complete the notarization.

87. Answer: b) No, never

Explanation: Notarizing a document for an individual who is not of sound mind violates notarial principles as the individual must have the capacity to understand the transaction.

88. Answer: c) Yes, under certain conditions

Explanation: A Notary Public may correct a notarial certificate or attach a correct notarial certificate if the original is missing or incorrect, assuming all other aspects of the notarization are compliant.

89. Answer: b) No, never

Explanation: A Notary Public must refuse to notarize if the signatory is not mentally competent, as competency is essential for the signatory to understand and engage in the transaction.

90. Answer: b) It must be typewritten or printed in black ink.

Explanation: Notarial certificates should be typewritten or printed in ink to ensure permanence and clarity. The color blue is often used for original signatures to distinguish originals from copies, but black ink is standard for the document text. There is no legal requirement for the document to be handwritten, signed by two witnesses, or written on legal-sized paper unless specified by the document or relevant legal stipulations.

91. Answer: c) The county where the document executes.

Explanation: Including the county where the document is executed in the heading of a notarial document is crucial for establishing the geographical jurisdiction within which the notarial act takes place, ensuring legal clarity and validity.

92. Answer: a) A statement of acknowledgment.

Explanation: A notarial document in New York must include a statement of acknowledgment, where the signer acknowledges before the Notary Public that they have signed the document voluntarily for its stated purpose.

93. Answer: b) False

Explanation: The notarial document is not required to contain the expiration date of the Notary's commission. While this information might be included as a best practice, it is not a statutory requirement for the validity of the notarization.

94. Answer: d) The signer must acknowledge the document.

Explanation: For a notarial document to be valid, the signer must personally appear before the Notary Public and acknowledge that the signature on the document is theirs and that the signing was done willingly.

95. Answer: c) The document must contain a sworn statement.

Explanation: When a notarial document includes a jurat, it indicates that the document contains a sworn statement by the signer, affirming the truthfulness of the document's content under penalty of perjury.

96. Answer: d) The notary public's seal.

Explanation: The notarial certificate of acknowledgment must include the Notary Public's seal, serving as a formal symbol of the Notary's authority and the authenticity of the notarization.

97. Answer: d) Jurisdictional stamp.

Explanation: In New York, a Notary Public must attach their jurisdictional stamp—or seal—to each notarial act performed, as it signifies the Notary's authority and the authenticity of the notarization.

98. Answer: b) False

Explanation: Backdating a notarial document is unethical and illegal, as it misrepresents the actual date of the notarial act, undermining the integrity of the notarization and potentially facilitating fraudulent activities.

100. Answer: b) The county where the notary's commission is registered.

Explanation: The county where the Notary's commission is registered is not a requirement to be included in the notarial certificate of acknowledgment. Essential elements typically include the date of notarization, the signature and printed name of the Notary, and the Notary's seal.

101. Answer: a) To record a formal declaration of non-payment or dishonor of negotiable instruments.

Explanation: A notarial certificate of protest is used to formally record the dishonor of negotiable instruments, such as checks or bills of exchange, verifying that payment was demanded and not received.

102. Answer: b) The corporate seal.

Explanation: For a corporate entity, the corporate seal, along with authorized signatures, is often required to execute notarial documents, symbolizing the corporation's legal and formal endorsement of the document.

103. Answer: b) False

Explanation: A Notary Public, irrespective of whether they are also an attorney, can issue a certificate of protest. The role does not necessitate legal qualifications beyond those required for a Notary Public.

104. Answer: d) To confirm the qualifications of a notary public.

Explanation: A notarial certificate of qualification verifies a Notary Public's current standing and authority to perform notarial acts, underscoring the legal basis for the Notary's actions.

105. Answer: c) The reason for the protest.

Explanation: The notarial certificate of protest must include the date and place of the protest and the signature of the Notary Public but does not necessarily require the reason for the protest as an essential element.

106. Answer: a) True

Explanation: A foundational principle of notarization is that the signer must be physically present before the Notary Public at the time of notarization to ensure proper identification and willingness to sign.

107. Answer: a) The notary public's commission expiration date.

Explanation: The notarial qualification certificate does not require the inclusion of the Notary Public's commission expiration date. Essential elements typically focus on the act of qualification itself.

108. Answer: d) To prove the execution of a document.

Explanation: A notarial certificate of proof is employed to verify that a document was executed by the signatory in a manner consistent with the legal requirements, ensuring the authenticity of the signer's participation.

109. Answer: b) False

Explanation: Not all documents related to real estate transactions necessitate a notarial certificate of proof. The requirement for such a certificate depends on the document type and the jurisdictional legal stipulations.

110. Answer: a) The notary public's seal.

Explanation: The notary public's seal is a critical element in the notarial certificate of proof, signifying the notarization's authenticity and the Notary's authority.

111. Answer: b) The document needs to be completed.

Explanation: A notary public may refuse to notarize a document if it is incomplete, as notarizing such a document could imply endorsement of incomplete or ambiguous content, potentially leading to fraud.

112. Answer: b) False

Explanation: A notary public cannot notarize their own signature due to the inherent conflict of interest and the principle of impartiality in notarization.

113. Answer: b) The date of the document's execution.

Explanation: In the notarial certificate of proof of execution, the inclusion of the date of the document's execution is essential, providing a temporal context for the notarial act.

114. Answer: c) To administer an oath or affirmation.

Explanation: The purpose of a notarial certificate of oath is to officially document the administration of an oath or affirmation by a Notary Public, ensuring that the individual taking the oath affirms the truthfulness of the information under penalty of perjury.

115. Answer: b) False

Explanation: While Notary Publics may charge fees for their services, the imposition of an extra fee specifically for attaching a certificate of authentication would depend on state regulations. Generally, notarial fees are standardized, and any additional charges must comply with legal guidelines.

116. Answer: d) The notary public's social security number.

Explanation: The inclusion of the Notary Public's social security number in the notarial certificate of oath is not a required element. Essential elements typically include the date of the oath, the signature of the Notary Public, and the printed name of the person taking the oath, ensuring proper identification and accountability.

117. Answer: c) To obtain permission for a minor to travel internationally.

Explanation: A notarial certificate of consent is commonly used to formally document a parent or legal guardian's consent for a minor to travel internationally, providing a legal basis for the travel arrangement in compliance with airline and immigration policies.

118. Answer: b) False

Explanation: A Notary Public must refuse to notarize a document that contains blank spaces to prevent fraudulent additions after the notarization has occurred. The document should be complete to ensure the integrity of the notarial act.

119. Answer: c) The signature of the person granting consent.

Explanation: The notarial certificate of consent must include the signature of the person granting consent, affirming the voluntary nature of the consent and providing a clear record of authorization.

120. Answer: c) Family law matters.

Explanation: Notarial certificates of consent are frequently utilized in family law matters, such as granting permission for a minor's international travel, reflecting the document's role in personal and family-related legal arrangements.

121. Answer: a) Refuse to notarize the document.

Explanation: A Notary Public should refuse to notarize a document when presented with an expired identification document, as the validity of the identification is crucial for verifying the signer's identity.

122. Answer: b) False

Explanation: A Notary Public cannot accept expired identification documents for notarization, regardless of the recentness of the expiration. Identification must be valid at the time of the notarial act.

123. Answer: a) Refuse to notarize the document.

Explanation: If a document lacks required elements, a Notary Public must refuse to notarize until all necessary information is provided and the document is complete, ensuring the legality and integrity of the notarial act.

124. Answer: c) Refuse to notarize the document until the blank spaces fill.

Explanation: A Notary Public should refuse to notarize a document containing blank spaces to prevent potential fraud or alterations, requiring the document to be fully completed before notarization.

125. Answer: b) False

Explanation: A Notary Public's role does not include determining the validity of a document's content; their responsibility is to verify the signer's identity and witness the signing, ensuring procedural correctness without assessing the document's legal validity.

126. Answer: c) Refuse to notarize the document and report the suspicious activity.

Explanation: Upon encountering a document that appears fraudulent or altered, a Notary Public should refuse to notarize and may report the suspicious activity to appropriate authorities, maintaining the notarial profession's integrity.

127. Answer: c) Refuse to notarize the document due to jurisdictional limitations.

Explanation: A Notary Public must operate within their jurisdictional boundaries. Notarizing documents executed in a different state or country could exceed their legal authority, requiring adherence to jurisdictional limitations.

128. Answer: b) False

Explanation: A Notary Public cannot make alterations or corrections to the substantive content of a completed document. Their role is to witness signings and authenticate identity, not to modify document content post-execution.

129. Answer: b) Decline to notarize the document and recommend finding a qualified translator.

Explanation: If a Notary Public cannot understand the language in which a document is written, they should decline to notarize due to the inability to accurately verify the document's contents, thereby ensuring the integrity of the notarial act.

130. Answer: b) Create a new notarial certificate and attach it to the document.

Explanation: Should a document lack a notarial certificate, a Notary Public may attach a correct certificate, provided they comply with the legal requirements for the notarial act being performed, ensuring the notarization's validity.

131. Answer: b) False

Explanation: A Notary Public should not certify a copy of an expired identification document as it no longer serves as valid proof of the signatory's identity, maintaining the standards of notarial practice.

132. Answer: b) Refuse to notarize the document until the missing signatures provide.

Explanation: A Notary Public must refuse to notarize a document lacking required signatures to prevent notarizing an incomplete legal document, thereby upholding the legality and completeness of the notarial act.

133. Answer: d) Refuse to notarize the document and recommend seeking legal advice.

Explanation: Upon encountering contradictory information in a document, a Notary Public should refuse to notarize and advise seeking legal counsel to resolve discrepancies, maintaining the document's integrity.

134. Answer: a) True

Explanation: A Notary Public can correct mistakes on a completed notarial certificate if they observe the error immediately, ensuring the correction is made properly and noted accordingly to maintain the record's accuracy.

135. Answer: d) Refuse to notarize the document and recommend consulting an attorney.

Explanation: A Notary Public must refuse to notarize a document signed by a deceased person as the individual cannot appear before the Notary or consent to the notarization, necessitating legal consultation.

136. Answer: c) Refuse to notarize the document and recommend seeking legal advice.

Explanation: If a Notary Public suspects a signer lacks the mental capacity to understand the document, they must refuse to notarize to ensure the signer's comprehension and voluntary participation, recommending legal guidance for further action.

137. Answer: a) True

Explanation: A Notary Public can notarize a document executed by a person with a power of attorney, provided the Notary verifies the signer's identity and authority to sign on behalf of the principal.

138. Answer: b) Refuse to notarize the document until the missing notarial act provides.

Explanation: A Notary Public must ensure all requirements for a notarial act are met before proceeding; if a required notarial act is missing, the Notary should refuse to notarize until the document is completed.

139. Answer: c) Refuse to notarize the document until the missing attachments or exhibits provide.

Explanation: Missing attachments or exhibits could contain critical information for the document; hence, a Notary should refuse to notarize until these components are presented to ensure the document's completeness.

140. Answer: b) False

Explanation: A Notary Public can notarize a document executed by someone who cannot sign using alternative methods approved by law, such as marking with an "X" in the presence of witnesses.

141. Answer: b) Decline to notarize the document and recommend resolving the conflict.

Explanation: When faced with conflicting instructions, a Notary Public should decline to notarize to avoid being implicated in potential disputes, recommending that the parties involved resolve their differences.

142. Answer: b) Refuse to notarize the document until it is complete.

Explanation: Notarizing an incomplete document could lead to fraudulent additions; thus, a Notary should only proceed once the document is fully completed.

143. Answer: b) False

Explanation: A Notary Public must ensure the signer understands the document's language to verify that they are fully aware of the content they are signing, emphasizing the importance of informed consent in notarial acts.

144. Answer: c) Refuse to notarize the document until the outdated or incorrect information is corrected.

Explanation: Notarizing a document with outdated or incorrect information could mislead or result in legal ambiguities, thereby necessitating correction prior to notarization.

145. Answer: a) Notarize the document and create a separate notarial certificate to attach.

Explanation: If a document is missing a notarial certificate, a Notary Public may prepare and attach the appropriate certificate, provided it meets the required criteria for the notarial act, ensuring the document's notarization proceeds correctly.

146. Answer: b) False

Explanation: A Notary Public is required to verify the identity of the signatory through acceptable means of identification. If a signer refuses to provide such identification, the Notary must refuse to notarize the document to uphold the integrity and legality of the notarial act.

147. Answer: c) Refuse to notarize the document and request clarification from the signer.

Explanation: Should a document contain conflicting information regarding the signer's identity, the Notary Public must refuse to proceed with the notarization until the discrepancies are resolved, ensuring the authenticity of the signer's identity.

148. Answer: c) Refuse to notarize the document until it is readable and clear.

Explanation: Notarizing a document that is illegible or contains indecipherable markings compromises the Notary's ability to understand the document fully. Therefore, the Notary should refuse to notarize until the document's contents are made clear and understandable.

149. Answer: b) False

Explanation: The fundamental requirement for notarization is the physical presence of the signer before the Notary at the time of the act. A Notary cannot notarize a document if the person who is supposed to sign the document is not physically present.

150. Answer: c) Refuse to notarize the document and recommend resolving the conflict.

Explanation: A Notary Public must refuse to notarize a document containing contradictory or conflicting notarial certificates to avoid legal ambiguities. The Notary should advise resolving the conflicts before proceeding with notarization.

151. Answer: a) A situation where the Notary Public has a personal or financial interest in the transaction or document notarized.

Explanation: A conflict of interest for a Notary Public arises when they have a personal or financial stake in the document's transaction, potentially compromising their impartiality and the integrity of the notarial act.

152. Answer: b) False

Explanation: Notarizing documents for family members and close friends where a personal or financial interest exists can create a conflict of interest. Notaries must disclose such relationships and, in many cases, should refrain from notarizing to maintain impartiality.

153. Answer: a) Disclose the conflict of interest and refuse to notarize the document.

Explanation: If a Notary Public has a personal or financial interest in a document, they must disclose this conflict and refuse to notarize to preserve the notarization's impartiality and integrity.

154. Answer: b) False

Explanation: A Notary Public should not notarize documents for a business in which they hold a financial stake due to the potential conflict of interest, which could undermine the impartiality required in notarial acts.

155. Answer: b) In all situations where a conflict of interest exists.

Explanation: A Notary Public is obligated to disclose any conflict of interest in all situations to ensure transparency and maintain the credibility and impartiality of the notarial process.

156. Answer: b) False

Explanation: Notarizing documents for one's employer, especially in a managerial position, can present a conflict of interest. The Notary must assess each situation for potential conflicts and refrain from notarizing if impartiality could be compromised.

157. Answer: a) Notify the appropriate authorities and report the incident.

Explanation: If a Notary inadvertently notarizes a document where a conflict of interest exists, they should report the incident to maintain professional integrity and seek to rectify the situation as per regulatory guidance.

158. Answer: b) False

Explanation: Notarizing a document for a business partner can constitute a conflict of interest, potentially compromising the Notary's impartiality. Such situations should be avoided to uphold the integrity of the notarization.

159. Answer: d) Refuse to notarize the document until the conflict of interest resolves.

Explanation: In the presence of uncertainty regarding a conflict of interest, a Notary Public should refuse to notarize the document to prevent potential compromise of their impartiality, until the conflict is clearly resolved.

160. Answer: b) False

Explanation: Notarizing documents for immediate family members can create a conflict of interest due to personal relationships. Unless explicitly allowed by law and with no personal interest, Notaries should avoid such notarizations.

161. Answer: c) Refuse to notarize the document due to the conflict of interest.

Explanation: Notarizing a document for a close friend can present a conflict of interest, especially if there's a potential benefit for the Notary. To maintain impartiality, it's advisable to refuse such notarizations.

162. Answer: a) True

Explanation: A Notary Public may notarize a document for a business competitor, provided there is no direct personal or financial interest in the transaction that would affect the Notary's impartiality. Each situation should be evaluated individually to ensure compliance with ethical standards.

163. Answer: b) Decline the gift and continue with the notarization.

Explanation: A Notary Public should maintain professional integrity and impartiality by declining any gifts or gratuities offered in exchange for notarial services to avoid any perception of bias or unethical behavior.

164. Answer: b) False

Explanation: Notarizing documents for close relatives can present a conflict of interest, especially if the Notary could stand to benefit from the transaction, even indirectly. Most jurisdictions advise against or prohibit such notarizations to preserve the notarization's integrity.

165. Answer: a) Disclose the conflict of interest and refuse to notarize the document.

Explanation: If a Notary Public has a financial interest in the property involved in a real estate transaction, they must disclose this conflict and recuse themselves from the notarization to prevent any potential bias or compromise of the notarial act's impartiality.

166. Answer: a) True

Explanation: A Notary Public can notarize a document for a client even if they have a personal relationship with the client's attorney, provided there is no direct financial interest or personal benefit from the transaction that could influence the Notary's impartiality.

167. Answer: b) Notify the appropriate authorities and seek legal advice.

Explanation: If a Notary Public becomes aware of a conflict of interest after completing a notarization, they should seek legal advice and notify any relevant authorities to address the situation appropriately and ensure compliance with notarial ethics and laws.

168. Answer: b) False

Explanation: Notarizing documents for a landlord or tenant can create a perceived conflict of interest, particularly if the Notary could benefit from the relationship, affecting the notarization's perceived impartiality.

169. Answer: a) Disclose the conflict of interest and offer to recuse themselves from the notarization.

Explanation: In situations where a Notary Public has a financial interest in a business that is a party to the document, they should disclose this conflict and recuse themselves to maintain the notarization's integrity and impartiality.

170. Answer: a) True

Explanation: A Notary Public can notarize documents for their employer's clients, provided the notarization does not involve a direct personal or financial interest that could impair the Notary's impartiality.

171. Answer: a) Proceed with the notarization but disclose the personal relationship.

Explanation: If a Notary Public has a personal relationship with the person requesting the notarization but no financial interest in the transaction, they may proceed with the notarization, ensuring transparency by disclosing the relationship.

172. Answer: b) False

Explanation: If a Notary Public has provided legal advice to a client, notarizing documents for the same client could present a conflict of interest, particularly if the legal advice relates to the document being notarized.

173. Answer: c) Refuse to notarize the document due to the conflict of interest.

Explanation: A Notary Public must refuse to notarize a document if they have a personal interest in the document, even if they are not a direct party to the transaction, to avoid any conflict of interest.

174. Answer: b) False

Explanation: Notarizing a document for a business entity in which the Notary holds stock could constitute a conflict of interest if the Notary stands to benefit from the notarization, thus compromising their impartiality.

175. Answer: a) Proceed with the notarization and disclose the personal relationship.

Explanation: A Notary Public may proceed with notarizing a document if they have a personal relationship with the signer but no financial interest in the document, provided they disclose the relationship to maintain transparency.

176. Answer: a) True

Explanation: A Notary Public can notarize a document for a client even if they have a personal relationship with the client's accountant, as long as the Notary does not have a direct financial interest in the transaction being notarized.

177. Answer: b) Refuse to notarize the document due to the conflict of interest.

Explanation: If a Notary Public has a financial interest in a document but is not a party to the transaction, they must refuse to notarize to avoid a conflict of interest, ensuring the notarial act remains impartial.

178. Answer: a) True

Explanation: A Notary Public can notarize documents for coworkers, provided the notarization does not involve transactions in which the Notary has a personal or financial interest, maintaining professional integrity.

179. Answer: a) Proceed with the notarization and disclose the friendship.

Explanation: If notarizing a document for a friend and the Notary Public does not have a personal or financial interest in the transaction, they may proceed but should disclose the relationship to ensure transparency.

180. Answer: a) True

Explanation: A Notary Public may notarize a document for a client if they have a personal relationship with the client's insurance agent, assuming there is no conflict of interest that could affect the Notary's impartiality in the notarization process.

181. Answer: a) Power of Attorney

Explanation: A Power of Attorney (PoA) document often necessitates an oath or affirmation administered by a Notary Public as part of its execution process. The requirement for such an oath or affirmation is due to the significant legal authority granted through the PoA, which allows the designated agent to act on behalf of the principal in various legal and financial matters. The oath or affirmation ensures that the principal acknowledges their understanding of the document's implications and the authority being granted, thereby enhancing the document's integrity and legal standing. In contrast, birth certificates and marriage licenses are typically issued by government agencies and do not require notarization for their initial issuance. Rental agreements may require notarization depending on jurisdictional requirements and the parties' preference but do not inherently necessitate an oath or affirmation as part of their execution.

182. Answer: c) To deter fraud or false statements.

Explanation: The primary purpose of administering an oath or affirmation by a Notary Public is to deter fraud and false statements by obligating the individual to affirm the truthfulness of their statements or documents under penalty of perjury, thus enhancing the legal accountability of the declarant.

183. Answer: a) Make sure the document signer understands the oath.

Explanation: When administering an oath, it is imperative that the Notary Public ensures the document signer fully comprehends the significance and implications of the oath being taken, thereby safeguarding the integrity of the sworn statement or affirmation.

184. Answer: d) The notary public should ask the document signer to raise their right hand.

Explanation: A common practice in administering an oath involves asking the document signer to raise their right hand, a gesture signifying the solemnity of the oath-taking process, although the specific requirements may vary by jurisdiction.

185. Answer: b) No, a notary public cannot administer an oath to themselves.

Explanation: A Notary Public cannot administer an oath to themselves as it constitutes a conflict of interest and undermines the notarial process's integrity, which is predicated on impartiality and the proper witnessing of oaths by a third party.

186. Answer: b) Certification verifies the accuracy of a document copy.

Explanation: The process of certification by a Notary Public involves verifying that a photocopy of a document is a true and accurate reproduction of the original document, thereby providing a layer of authenticity to the copy.

187. Answer: b) Compare the copy to the original document.

Explanation: When certifying a document copy, a Notary Public is required to meticulously compare the copy with the original document to ensure that the copy is a faithful and accurate reproduction, without alterations or omissions.

188. Answer: d) All of the above

Explanation: Typically, Notaries Public cannot certify copies of official documents such as driver's licenses, Social Security cards, and birth certificates, as these are considered vital records and are subject to specific regulations that often restrict such certifications to the issuing agency.

189. Answer: b) No, certification can only be done for physical copies.

Explanation: A Notary Public traditionally certifies physical document copies because verifying the authenticity of electronic documents and ensuring they are true copies pose unique challenges that differ from those associated with paper documents.

190. Answer: a) With their official stamp and signature.

Explanation: When certifying a document, a Notary Public must sign and apply their official stamp or seal to the certification, thereby validating the certification process with their official notarial mark and signature.

191. Answer: b) No, translation certification requires a separate translator.

Explanation: A Notary Public cannot certify a translation unless they are qualified as a translator in the languages involved. Translation certification typically requires verification by a professional translator who attests to the accuracy of the translation.

192. Answer: a) "I swear to tell the truth, the whole truth, and nothing but the truth."

Explanation: This statement exemplifies an oath administered by a Notary Public, wherein the individual affirms their commitment to truthfulness in their statements or attestations, underscoring the oath's role in upholding legal and ethical standards.

193. Answer: a) Yes, as long as it conveys the same meaning.

Explanation: A Notary Public may alter the wording of an oath as necessary, provided that the revised wording faithfully conveys the oath's original intent and meaning, ensuring that the solemn affirmation of truthfulness is maintained.

194. Answer: d) None

Explanation: Administering an oath typically does not require the presence of witnesses; the essential components involve the Notary Public and the individual taking the oath, focusing on the individual's affirmation of truthfulness.

195. Answer: a) Yes, as long as the document signer is physically present in New York.

Explanation: Remote notarization, including administering oaths via video conference, is permissible under specific legal frameworks that accommodate remote notarial acts, provided all regulatory requirements are met, including jurisdictional stipulations.

196. Answer: b) The document must be notarized.

Explanation: The requirement for notarization is not a prerequisite for administering an oath; rather, administering an oath is a distinct notarial act that can be performed independently of the document's notarization.

197. Answer: a) Make a note on the copy indicating it is a certified true copy.

Explanation: When certifying a document copy, a Notary Public is required to clearly indicate on the copy that it has been certified as a true and accurate reproduction of the original document, ensuring clarity and authenticity of the certification.

198. Answer: d) No, a document cannot be notarized more than once.

Explanation: Once a document has been notarized, it signifies that the notarial act has been completed and the document's signer's identity, willingness, and awareness have been verified at that time. Certifying a document that is already notarized is redundant and unnecessary, as the original notarization already serves to authenticate the signer's execution of the document.

199. Answer: c) Certification requires the document signer to take an oath.

Explanation: This statement is incorrect in the context of certifying a document's copy. Certification by a notary public involves verifying that a photocopy of a document is a true and accurate reproduction of the original document. It does not typically require the document signer to take an oath. The correct understanding is that certification attests to the authenticity of the document copy and does not necessarily guarantee the accuracy of the document contents nor is it limited by time or only applicable to government-issued documents.

200. Answer: b) No, a notary public must understand the document they certify.

Explanation: A notary public should not certify a document written in a language they do not understand because they cannot be certain of the document's content or context. Certifying a document requires the notary to ascertain certain facts about the document, which is not feasible without comprehending the text, thereby ensuring the notary acts within their knowledge and authority.

201. Answer: c) To deter fraudulent behavior.

Explanation: The primary purpose of administering an oath or affirmation in the notarial process is to deter fraudulent behavior by compelling the document signer to affirm the truthfulness of the information contained within the document under penalty of perjury, thus enhancing the document's integrity and the legal accountability of the signer.

202. Answer: d) By using their official signature.

Explanation: When certifying a document copy, a notary public should use their official signature, which is registered with the notary's governing body. This signature, along with the notary's official seal or stamp, formalizes the certification, indicating that the notary has verified the copy as a true and accurate reproduction of the original document.

203. Answer: d) All of the above.

Explanation: When certifying a document copy, a notary public may need to perform several actions to complete the certification properly. This includes dating and signing the document, attaching a notarial certificate that states the document is a true copy, and applying a special seal if required by jurisdictional laws, thereby ensuring the document's certification is comprehensively documented and authenticated.

204. Answer: c) Yes, for both administering an oath and certification of documents.

Explanation: Notary publics are permitted to charge fees for their services, which can include administering oaths or affirmations and certifying document copies. The fees that a notary public can charge for these services are often regulated by state law to ensure they are reasonable and accessible.

205. Answer: c) Start over with a new document copy.

Explanation: If a mistake is made in a certified document copy, the most appropriate and professional action is to start the certification process over with a new document copy. This ensures the accuracy and integrity of the certified copy, as alterations or corrections on the certified copy could raise questions about its authenticity.

206. Answer: a) Last will.

Explanation: A last will is a legal document that may require notarization or witnesses to the signing to ensure its validity, depending on jurisdictional requirements. Notary publics might certify signatures on a last will or administer oaths to witnesses, reinforcing the document's legal standing and the signer's intent.

207. Answer: a) Refuse to notarize the document.

Explanation: If a document signer refuses to take an oath or affirmation when such is required by the notarial act, the notary public must refuse to notarize the document. Administering an oath is a critical step for certain notarial acts to affirm the truthfulness of the signer's statements, and without it, the notary cannot proceed in good conscience or in compliance with notarial standards.

208. Answer: b) No, a notary public should not certify confidential documents.

Explanation: A notary public has a responsibility to maintain the confidentiality and integrity of the documents they handle. Certifying a document that contains confidential information without proper authorization or legal grounds could potentially violate privacy laws or ethical guidelines. Therefore, notaries should exercise caution and avoid certifying documents that could compromise confidentiality.

209. Answer: d) They should use an alternative method to affirm the oath.

Explanation: If a document signer cannot physically raise their right hand for an oath due to a disability or injury, the notary public should adapt the oath administration process to accommodate the signer's physical limitations. This could involve using an alternative gesture or verbally affirming the oath, ensuring that the essential purpose of the oath—to commit the signer to truthfulness—is still achieved.

210. Answer: d) No, certification requires the inspection of the original document.

Explanation: Certification by a notary public involves attesting that a copy of a document is a true and accurate reproduction of the original. Without the original document for comparison, a notary cannot verify the accuracy of the copy. Therefore, the presence of the original document is crucial for the certification process.

211. Answer: b) Ensuring document confidentiality

Explanation: Document management techniques in notary practice are primarily concerned with ensuring the confidentiality and security of the documents handled. This includes proper storage, handling, and disposal methods to protect sensitive information and maintain the trust of clients.

212. Answer: c) Using a secure, locked filing system

Explanation: Recommended practice for document storage in a notary office involves using a secure, locked filing system to protect sensitive information and ensure confidentiality. This method prevents unauthorized access and helps maintain the integrity of the documents.

213. Answer: c) 3 years

Explanation: While retention periods can vary depending on jurisdiction and the type of document, a common practice is for notaries to retain copies of notarized documents or records of notarial acts for at least 3 years. This period allows for adequate record-keeping and accountability.

214. Answer: c) Encrypting them when transmitting electronically.

Explanation: When handling sensitive or confidential documents, especially in digital form, encrypting the documents during transmission is essential to protect the information from unauthorized access or interception, ensuring the confidentiality and integrity of the documents.

215. Answer: d) Shredding the documents using a cross-cut shredder

Explanation: A secure method of document disposal involves shredding the documents using a cross-cut shredder, which cuts the paper both vertically and horizontally, making it extremely difficult to reconstruct the documents. This method helps protect sensitive information from being compromised.

216. Answer: c) Encrypting the backup to protect sensitive information

Explanation: When making a backup of digital documents, it is crucial to encrypt the backup to ensure that sensitive information is protected. Encryption adds a layer of security that safeguards the data from unauthorized access or breaches.

217. Answer: a) To track changes made to records over time

Explanation: Implementing version control for notary documents allows notaries to track changes made to records over time. This practice is vital for maintaining the accuracy and integrity of documents, ensuring that all modifications are documented and retrievable.

218. Answer: c) Regular system backups and disaster recovery plan

Explanation: An essential feature of a secure document management system includes having regular system backups and a comprehensive disaster recovery plan. These measures are critical for ensuring data integrity and availability, protecting against data loss due to system failures, cyber-attacks, or natural disasters.

219. Answer: c) Information about a record, such as the author, creation date, and file size,

Explanation: In document management, "metadata" refers to data that provides information about other data, such as the author, creation date, and file size of a document. Metadata plays a crucial role in organizing, managing, and retrieving documents efficiently.

220. Answer: c) Grouping documents by date, category, or client name.

Explanation: The recommended approach for organizing and labeling physical documents involves grouping them by specific criteria, such as date, category, or client name. This systematic method enhances the efficiency of document retrieval and management, ensuring that records are easily accessible and well-organized.

221. Answer: b) Reject the document and request a new, undamaged copy.

Explanation: A notary public must ensure the document's integrity before notarization. If a document is damaged or altered, it could compromise the document's legality and the notarization's validity. Thus, requesting a new, undamaged copy ensures the notarization process adheres to legal standards and maintains document integrity.

222. Answer: b) Increased risk of unauthorized access or interception.

Explanation: Sharing digital documents via email exposes the documents to risks of unauthorized access or interception by third parties. Email transmissions, especially if unencrypted, can be vulnerable to hacking, phishing attacks, or interception, compromising the confidentiality and security of the information contained in the documents.

223. Answer: c) Use a secure bag or briefcase designed for document transport.

Explanation: When transporting physical documents off-site, it is paramount to ensure their security and confidentiality. Using a secure bag or briefcase designed specifically for document transport minimizes the risk of loss, theft, or unauthorized access, thus protecting sensitive information.

224. Answer: a) Restricting access to only authorized individuals.

Explanation: Access controls in document management play a crucial role in securing sensitive information by ensuring that only authorized individuals have access to specific documents. This mechanism protects against unauthorized viewing, alteration, or distribution, thereby preserving document confidentiality and integrity.

225. Answer: b) Storing documents in multiple physical locations.

Explanation: Storing documents in multiple physical locations is a recommended practice for preventing document loss. This approach provides redundancy, ensuring that if one storage location is compromised due to disasters, theft, or other unforeseen circumstances, backup copies of the documents remain safe elsewhere.

226. Answer: b) To establish guidelines for document storage and retention.

Explanation: Implementing a document retention policy is essential for outlining how long documents should be kept and the procedures for their storage and eventual disposal. This policy helps organizations manage their records efficiently, comply with legal requirements, and ensure the timely destruction of outdated or unnecessary documents.

227. Answer: a) Keep them secure and return them promptly after notarization.

Explanation: Notaries must treat original documents provided by clients with the utmost care, keeping them secure during the notarization process and returning them promptly afterward. This practice ensures the documents' safety and respects the client's ownership and confidentiality.

228. Answer: a) PDF (Portable Document Format).

Explanation: PDF is a commonly used digital document format in notary practice due to its wide acceptance, ability to preserve document formatting across different platforms, and options for securing documents with features such as passwords and digital signatures.

229. Answer: c) Implement strong passwords and access controls.

Explanation: Protecting digital documents from unauthorized access is critical. Implementing strong passwords and access controls helps secure digital document storage, preventing unauthorized access and maintaining the confidentiality and integrity of the documents.

230. Answer: c) Dropbox.

Explanation: Dropbox is an example of a cloud-based document management system that allows users to store, share, and access documents remotely. Cloud-based systems offer flexibility, accessibility, and options for collaboration while maintaining data security through encryption and access controls.

231. Answer: c) By implementing digital signatures or electronic seals.

Explanation: The integrity of electronic documents can be ensured through the use of digital signatures or electronic seals, which provide a secure method of authenticating the identity of the document signer and the document's unaltered status since the time of signing.

232. Answer: b) Reject the document and notify the relevant authorities.

Explanation: If a notary suspects a document has been tampered with, they should refuse to notarize it and notify relevant authorities if necessary. This approach prevents the potential legalization of fraudulent or altered documents, maintaining the notarization process's integrity.

233. Answer: b) Keep a record of all versions and revisions.

Explanation: Maintaining a record of all document versions and revisions is crucial for tracking changes over time, ensuring transparency, and preserving the document's history. This practice allows for accountability and verification of the document's evolution.

234. Answer: c) Notify all parties involved and rectify the mistake promptly.

Explanation: If a notary accidentally notarizes the wrong document, they must immediately inform all involved parties of the mistake and take appropriate steps to rectify the error, maintaining professional responsibility and credibility.

235. Answer: c) Regularly reviewing and purging outdated documents.

Explanation: A best practice in document management involves regularly reviewing and purging outdated documents, which helps manage storage space efficiently, ensures compliance with retention policies, and reduces the risk of unauthorized access to obsolete or sensitive information.

236. Answer: b) To establish protocols for document restoration after a disaster.

Explanation: Implementing a disaster recovery plan for document management is essential for establishing protocols to restore documents and maintain business continuity after a disaster. This plan outlines steps for data recovery, securing backup copies, and minimizing the impact of disasters on document accessibility and integrity.

237. Answer: b) Refrain from notarizing the document until all necessary information is provided.

Explanation: A notary should not proceed with notarization if a document contains missing or incomplete information, as this could impact the document's legality or validity. The notary must ensure all required information is present before performing the notarial act.

238. Answer: c) Shred them using a cross-cut shredder.

Explanation: When physical documents are no longer needed and are to be disposed of, shredding them using a cross-cut shredder is a secure method to prevent unauthorized access to or recovery of sensitive information, ensuring the confidentiality and privacy of the information contained in the documents.

239. Answer: a) To create an organized and searchable database of documents.

Explanation: Document indexing in a notary office serves to systematically organize documents in a way that makes them easily searchable and retrievable. This process enhances efficiency and accessibility, allowing notaries and their clients to quickly locate specific documents or information when needed.

240. Answer: b) Encrypt them before transmitting or storing them digitally.

Explanation: Handling documents that contain personally identifiable information (PII) demands stringent security measures to protect against unauthorized access or breaches. Encrypting these documents before their transmission or digital storage ensures the confidentiality and integrity of the PII, safeguarding individuals' privacy.

241. Answer: d) Fee for providing legal advice.

Explanation: Notary Publics are authorized to charge fees for specific notarial acts such as administering oaths and taking acknowledgments. However, providing legal advice falls outside the scope of a Notary's duties and, therefore, cannot be subject to a fee by a Notary Public. Notaries must refrain from offering legal advice unless they are also licensed attorneys.

242. Answer: b) Notary Publics must securely store personal information.

Explanation: The collection of personal information during notarization processes places a responsibility on Notary Publics to securely store this information. This duty aims to protect the privacy and confidentiality of the individuals' personal data, preventing unauthorized access and potential misuse.

243. Answer: a) Yes, but only if required by law.

Explanation: A Notary Public may only disclose personal information obtained during notarization to third parties without the client's consent if such disclosure is mandated by law. This condition ensures that personal information is handled with confidentiality, except when legal obligations necessitate disclosure.

244. Answer: c) 5 years.

Explanation: While the specific retention period for personal information collected during notarization may vary by jurisdiction, a general guideline is to retain this information for a significant period, such as 5 years, to comply with legal requirements and for record-keeping purposes.

245. Answer: a) Yes, but only if encrypted and password-protected.

Explanation: Storing personal information electronically is permissible for a Notary Public, provided that stringent security measures, such as encryption and password protection, are implemented. These precautions ensure the security and confidentiality of the personal information against unauthorized access.

246. Answer: a) Shredding or permanently deleting the information.

Explanation: Secure disposal of personal information is crucial to protecting individuals' privacy. Shredding physical documents or permanently deleting electronic records are effective methods to ensure that personal information is irretrievably destroyed, mitigating risks of unauthorized access or misuse.

247. Answer: c) No, personal information cannot be used for marketing purposes.

Explanation: Using personal information obtained during notarization for marketing purposes without explicit consent violates privacy principles and ethical standards governing Notary Publics. Such information must be used solely for the purposes of notarization and related official duties.

248. Answer: c) No, additional personal information should not be requested.

Explanation: A Notary Public should only request personal information from the client that is necessary for the completion of the notarization process. Soliciting additional, unnecessary personal information is inappropriate and could infringe on the individual's privacy.

249. Answer: a) Immediately notify the affected individuals and appropriate authorities.

Explanation: In the event of a suspected data breach or unauthorized access to personal information, a Notary Public has an obligation to promptly inform the affected individuals and relevant authorities. This response helps mitigate potential harm and complies with legal requirements concerning data breaches.

250. Answer: a) Store them in a locked cabinet or secure location.

Explanation: After notarization, physical documents containing personal information should be stored in a secure manner, such as in a locked cabinet or another secure location. This practice ensures the documents' safety and confidentiality, protecting personal information from unauthorized access or misuse.

Conclusion

As we conclude this comprehensive guide on becoming a New York Notary Public, it's essential to reflect on the journey we've embarked upon together. From the historical roots of notaries in New York, dating back to the colonial era, to the intricacies of passing the Notary Public Exam, this guide has aimed to equip you with the knowledge and skills necessary for success in this vital role.

The role of a notary in New York is both noble and demanding, serving as the bedrock of legal transactions and the authenticity of documents. We've explored the significance of the exam, highlighting its role in demonstrating a candidate's mastery of legal and ethical responsibilities. Successful completion of the exam is not just a personal achievement; it's a commitment to upholding the integrity and efficiency of New York's legal system.

This guide has underscored the eligibility criteria set forth by the state, including age, residency, and citizenship requirements, alongside the criticality of a clean criminal background. These prerequisites ensure that only those with the utmost integrity and responsibility are granted the honor of serving as notaries.

Moreover, we've delved into practical strategies for exam preparation, from time and stress management to the utilization of study groups and mentors. The exam's scope, covering notary laws, duties, ethics, and procedures, demands thorough preparation and a deep understanding of the notary's role in society.

In mastering the content outlined in this guide, you are now well-equipped to embark on your journey as a notary public in New York, ready to face the challenges and fulfill the responsibilities that come with this esteemed position.

As we close this chapter, I want to extend my deepest gratitude to you, the reader, for choosing this guide as your companion on the path to becoming a Notary Public in New York. Your dedication to serving the public and upholding the law is commendable, and I wish you every success in your future endeavors as a notary. Thank you for embarking on this journey with us.

Made in United States
Orlando, FL
31 August 2024

50962629R00063